THE SECRET TO PROSPERITY

Awaken Your Passion, Achieve Success and
Become Wealthy

By Marc Hill

DEDICATION

For my parents, you have always been there for me.
I love you both and owe you everything.

DISCLAIMER

This book does not claim to provide financial, legal or health care advice. The material written in this book is for informational purposes only. This book does not offer advice regarding the nature, value or suitability of any particular investment strategy. Everyone's financial situation is different. Particular investment strategies mentioned in this book may not be suitable for you. All investments carry risk and past results do not guarantee future performance. The information in this book are only suggestions and it is up to the reader to make his or her own decisions. Consult with a certified financial advisor or healthcare professional when evaluating any material in this book.

CONTENTS

ACKNOWLEDGEMENTS

I would like to thank M.J. Hill, Mac Hill, Darold Gholston, Bob Brazelton and Nick Brown for their encouragement while writing this book.

INTRODUCTION
By Mac Hill

There comes a time in each of our lives when we must make a pivotal decision. You must decide to acknowledge your inner flame. The flame within your soul is not satisfied with living a life of mediocrity. No matter how much you ignore it, this flame will not go away because you are hardwired for greatness. There is a dynamic life waiting for you! There is no obstacle that can prevent you from actualizing your greatness. This book will show you how to become the limitless person you are destined to be. Success, fulfillment, and financial freedom will be yours.

However, figuratively speaking, you must stand outside of yourself and make a realistic evaluation of your makeup. Are you willing to do what it takes and walk the extra mile to accomplish your purpose in life? Do you have the discipline to pick up your feet and forge ahead when the going gets tough? Finally, you must have the willingness to remove excuses from your conscious thoughts when each day requires you to be optimistic and move forward. Reading this book will definitely help you make the right decision toward understanding why you need to take a long look in the mirror and decide whether you will take the weak and unprofitable path laid out before you or plow through a new, tough and more dynamic path.

By grasping the concepts in this book, you will examine and internalize methods to gain an unwavering insight into how to structure your own independent thinking. You will not be afraid of failure. Adversity will be your path to success. You will learn, specifically, how to multiply your money and how others were able to monetize their passions to create financial independence.

You will learn how to live in the moment of doing better and being the very best you can be. You will learn the principles of eating to live and how nutrition correlates to personal achievement. You will begin to focus on the new you and what you want out of life. This is not just a feel good book about positive thinking and waiting for your dreams to magically become reality. This book is action oriented! You will be given concrete ideas, solutions, and tactics about how to bring dynamic change into your life for the better.

THE SECRET TO PROSPERITY

CHAPTER 1

AS YOU THINK, YOU SHALL BECOME

You were born limitless and have infinite capabilities. All accomplishments originate as a thought. Your life is currently a reflection of your innermost thoughts. Your thoughts will continue to attract everything that comes to fruition in your life. If you want to improve your life, then you must improve your thoughts. You are guaranteed to achieve whatever you want if you keep your mind focused. No external force can stand in your way.

The Power of Visualization

Your imagination is what creates reality. There are no limits on your life because there are no limits on your imagination. What you consistently visualize in your mind will eventually materialize in your life. Everything you see in the physical world was once an unseen thought in someone's mind. Before the Empire State Building was built, it was first visualized in an architect's imagination. Before Neil Armstrong set foot on the moon, administrators at NASA imagined and believed it was possible for a human to explore our galaxy. This is the process for any achievement in life. The primary reason most people never achieve their dreams is because they don't have the proper vision. Most people don't have any vision at all. Many people find it difficult to visualize greatness because they do not understand the process of how their dreams will materialize.

Never worry about the mechanics of how your dreams will come to fruition. As long as you continually indoctrinate your goals into your subconscious mind, the universe will lead you towards opportunities and people that will help bring them to reality. Proper visualization takes practice and effort. You must consistently weed out negative thoughts and distractions. The more you do it, the easier it will get. Every day you must imagine your life as if you have already achieved the goals you desire. Imagine you are already the person you want to become. What you envision will shape your reality. Never underestimate the power of imagery. What you see in your mind's eye is so powerful that corporations annually spend millions of dollars on advertising to shape the image they want you to identify as their brand. Many celebrities have sleepless nights worrying about how their public images are viewed by the masses. They understand that the way you see them in your mind's eye will have a profound effect on their earnings. What you envision about yourself will also have a profound effect on your success. You should get in the habit of visualizing your major goals at least once every day. Repetitive imagery is powerful. Any seed constantly nourished in your mind will eventually grow and produce results. Once you combine your imagination with faith and action, you will be destined for success.

Extreme Desire

When you really want something, you will certainly find a way to achieve it. You will go into a zone where obstacles such as fear, pain, and excuses will be nonexistent. You will run on autopilot in a steady path towards your prize. If you truly desire to achieve your goal, it is literally guaranteed you will have it. People say they want many things, but they don't have the desire! You must have a burning passion for what you want. You must want to achieve your objective as if your life depends on it. As time passes, the light at the end of the tunnel will become brighter. You will begin to magnetize opportunities and good fortune effortlessly. The secret to reaching your goals in life is to have sincere desire.

The next step is to take action. When a baby desires to walk, he or she has to crawl first. A baby will stumble many times, but will never quit. A baby doesn't have fear, isn't scared of failure and doesn't make excuses. A baby has a burning desire to walk. Adults can learn a lot from children. We are so busy trying to teach kids, we miss the valuable lessons they are teaching us.

Fight against mediocrity. Everyone has the potential to be extraordinary. Never lose your childlike ambition and fearlessness. Never allow fear or excuses to deter you from accomplishing your dreams. Where there is a strong will, there is always a way. If you can't find a way, then create a way. Raise your standards and never become complacent.

When the Wright brothers dreamed of the possibility of man flying like a bird, they had not the foggiest idea of how their idea would become reality. In the beginning, they didn't know how to successfully manufacture an airplane. The Wright brothers were bicycle mechanics who had not graduated high school. Despite the odds, they stayed dedicated and through trial and error the answers eventually became evident. Persistence and faith make dreams come true. Just believe, get to work and the answers will come.

Sacrifice and Pay the Price

He who would accomplish little need sacrifice little, he who would achieve much must sacrifice much. He who would attain highly must sacrifice greatly.- James Allen

Sacrifice is paramount when it comes to accomplishing greatness. If you want to lose weight and get in shape, then you have to sacrifice junk food. Everything worth achieving has a price up front. When you sacrifice bad habits long enough, you eventually forget you had them. Living without bad habits will feel normal in time. If you want to become debt free then you have to decrease your consumption and sell unnecessary possessions. If you want to become a medical doctor, then you will need to sacrifice many parties and social events to study more on the weekends. Sacrificing is vital when you want to make gains.

Learn how to embrace being uncomfortable in the beginning. If you lift weights for the first time your muscles will be sore the next morning. The soreness means your muscles are getting stronger. The pain and soreness will go away the more you keep working out. The more you push, the faster the pain will go away. Billionaire Elon Musk had to sacrifice during his early days as an entrepreneur. Since money was scarce, he kept expenses low and lived in his small PayPal startup office. He took showers at the local YMCA. His sacrifice and dedication eventually paid off. PayPal was sold to eBay for $1.6 billion in 2002. Achieving any worthy goal will be strenuous upfront, but the adversity always makes for a sweeter victory in the end.

Fail, Learn and Keep Moving

If you never quit, you cannot fail. Champions are not those who never fail, but those who never quit. Stay in until you win. - Edwin Cole

Mistakes are learning lessons that will make you wiser. Mastery comes from the accumulation of many lessons learned. Failure is a part of the process of achieving success. You automatically grow and learn when you make errors. For every error you make, you are getting one step closer to finding out what will work. Many people are afraid of failure because they think failure will define them as a person or hurt their image. This is far from reality. A failure is only a single event just as an achievement is a single event. One achievement or one failure does not define you. Wins and losses are nothing but experiences that are both needed like yin and yang. An achievement simply gives you more confidence that you are capable of accomplishing your goals. Adversity should make you even more determined and passionate about your vision. You have to crawl before you walk and an occasional stumble is just a natural part of the process.

Most setbacks are blessings in disguise. Most failures bring awareness to other strategies or pathways that are more suited to bringing your vision to reality in the most efficient way. When a certain relationship or business opportunity does not work out, it is usually the universe pushing you towards a better relationship or more lucrative business opportunity. I have seen people who were very depressed after a failed relationship. A few months later they were happier than ever with a new companion. The universe had something better in store.

I remember when I lost a silent auction bid on a beautiful house in an upscale community. I was disappointed at first, but the universe had something better in store for me. I began to realize that I really did not need to own a house at that time in my life. I took the money I had saved for a down payment on a house and started investing in the stock market. I always casually followed the market, but my unsuccessful bid on the house sparked me to get really serious about increasing my wealth. The lessons I learned from investing are priceless. A few years later I quadrupled my capital through saving and investing. If I had won the bid on that house, I would have been "house" poor like the masses. I would have sunk a lot of energy and the majority of my money into upgrading and maintaining the home. I would not have had the motivation or the extra capital to invest in stocks. My failure to win the bid on that house ended up being a blessing.

You should become excited with every new challenge. Adversity builds character and strength.

You sharpen a knife's blade with the friction of rubbing it along a steel rod. If you want to become sharper, then you should welcome pressure and adversity. The tougher the battle, the sweeter the victory.

When a professional football team wins the Super Bowl, nobody cares about how many games were lost during the season. When a Quarterback makes it to the hall of fame, nobody cares about how many interceptions he threw in his career. Hall of Fame baseball player Reggie Jackson accomplished many feats during his career. He was a 14x All-Star, 5x World Series champion, 2x World Series MVP, and 4x AL home run leader. Reggie Jackson hit 563 career home runs. Fans celebrate his achievements. Nobody cares that he had 2,597 strikeouts. He became a legendary player because he was not afraid to fail. He knew that if he kept swinging, he would eventually hit a home run.

If you keep swinging in life, you will also hit plenty of home runs. Learn from your mistakes and don't repeat them. Also, learn from other people's mistakes. It saves you valuable time and agony. Follow the winning trail to success. Learn from how other people overcame adversity. Winning habits that work for others will also work for you.

Enjoy the Journey

Enjoy the road to prosperity. Too often people are in a rush to get to the finish line and don't enjoy the process. There is no reason to be impatient. As long as you are making progress, you are already successful. When you achieve one goal, there will always be another goal to set. It is natural to continue growing. Nature dictates that you are either getting better or worse. A tree must continue to grow or it will die. The goal setting process is never ending so you may as well enjoy the journey. When you listen to your favorite song, you don't fast forward and rush to the end. The best part is somewhere in the middle. Enjoy the process and let it play through. If you take a road trip across country, from New York to California, the majority of the fun is enjoying the scenic view of the countryside and stopping in different cities along the way. This is the same way we should enjoy the pursuit of our dreams. The prize is in the process. The best part about pursuing prosperity is in the wisdom you will acquire, interesting people you will meet and the small victories along the way.

Long Term Thinking is Powerful

Mediocre people only make plans for the weekend. Extraordinary people make plans for their great-grandchildren. Think like a great chess player who is always looking three or four moves into the future. You can celebrate and learn from the past, but never dwell or live in it. There is a reason the front windshield of a car is bigger than the rearview mirror. Drivers would never reach their destinations safely if they continually focus on the rearview mirror. The front windshield is bigger because you are supposed to be looking forward most of the time. Live in the moment, but always plan for the future. Long-term thinking is why billionaire investor Warren Buffet is so successful. He is famous for being a long-term investor in stocks. When the economy is in a recession, most people are only thinking about the present moment. They panic and sell assets at low prices. Investors like Warren Buffet understand that for every dark day, the Sun will eventually shine again. They buy assets at cheap prices in the face of turmoil, and eventually make huge profits in the future when the economy recovers.

Automobile companies don't just design a car for the current year. They have a pipeline of concept vehicles ready for decades in the future. Auto companies are eager to display their futuristic cars at annual auto shows. They are always ahead of the curve. You must also stay ahead of the curve with a pipeline of goals decades in the future. The momentum of your personal progress should never stop. It is natural to have regrets about things you could have done differently in the past, but it is imperative that you bury previous disappointments. Everyone has something they wish they could go back in time and change. Since nobody has invented a time machine, there is no use in worrying about something you can't change. Let it go. If you made a bad investment, just let it go. If you were in a bad relationship, just let it go. If a business venture did not succeed, then just let it go and try again!

Successful athletes, let the past stay in the past. After a game is over, they'll watch the film, learn from their mistakes and quickly move on to prepare for their next opponent. The quicker you are able to move forward and focus on the next task, the more successful you will be. Remember that today is the first day of the rest of your life.

CHAPTER 2

WINNERS ARE PERSISTENT

Self-discipline is the ability to make yourself do what you should do, when you should do it, whether you feel like it or not. - Elbert Hubbard

When you are persistent and patient, you are unstoppable. Perseverance signifies that no matter what challenge or obstacle comes in your path you will adhere to the principles that will catapult you toward the attainment of your goal. You must stay the course, even if it seems like you are not making progress. Do something towards your goal every day. Small daily gains add up to phenomenal results over time. You will eventually build a castle if you stack one brick at a time. Remember the work is not over after your castle is built. When you plant a garden that produces tasty food, you cannot rest and think the job is done. You constantly have to maintain the garden or the weeds will choke out your nutritional harvest. Having the self-discipline to be consistent is the key. There is always room for improvement no matter how much greatness you achieve.

World renown actor Arnold Schwarzenegger

developed a strong work ethic at a young age. He was required to do sit-ups every morning to earn his breakfast. This taught Arnold how to persevere through temporary pain in order to achieve his goals. His disciplined work ethic followed him throughout his careers in bodybuilding, acting, business and politics. His persistence and self-discipline helped him reach the pinnacle of success in four different professions.

Persistence and Patience

There is no such thing as an overnight success. If you research any business icon or celebrity, you will find that it took many years of work to reach their current level of success. You will find that successful people are very persistent.

Consistent practice will eventually make you an expert over time. Embrace the fact that it may take 5 to 10 years of consistent effort before you realize substantial progress. Victory cannot be achieved instantly. Patience and perseverance is what converts an average person into an extraordinary achiever.

The Wright brothers endured a lot of difficulty before they invented the world's first successful airplane. They stayed persistent and never quit despite the odds. Tiger Woods started playing Golf at the age of 3 years old. He had almost 20 years of constant practice before he was ranked as the number one golfer in the world in 1997.

Phil Jackson, who coached Michael Jordan won 11 NBA titles as a coach. During Phil Jackson's early coaching career, he had to coach in a lower-level professional league in Puerto Rico. He was turned down many times for NBA coaching jobs. Phil Jackson never became discouraged and quit. He continued to hone his coaching skills in lower-level leagues for years. His consistency paid off by earning him the opportunity to coach the Chicago Bulls to six championships and the L.A. Lakers to five titles.

The Wright brothers, Tiger Woods, and Phil Jackson all developed an expertise in their chosen fields. Once you become known as an expert, money and success will follow. The only way to develop expertise is through patience and consistent practice.

Learn patience from how a bamboo tree grows. A bamboo tree grows very slowly and will not show any signs of growth above ground for the first 3 to 5 years. The tree actually makes a lot of progress underground by growing strong roots to create a firm foundation. When it finally surfaces above ground, it will grow rapidly up to 80 feet in as little as 6 weeks. Persistence will defeat all hardships. Harsh conditions don't last, but persistent people will. Stay determined and victory is guaranteed.

Growing Forever

Even if you're on the right track, you'll get run over if you just sit there. – Will Rogers

Never lose enthusiasm and drive after you have reached your goals. A person must continue to set higher goals. There is always more you can achieve. It is dangerous to rest on your laurels. Progression is the key to happiness. Always keep the ball moving forward. Stay dedicated to improving your intelligence, finances, health, etc. Nobody would have told Picasso to stop painting and improving as an artist. You would not tell the engineers at Ferrari to stop improving the design and efficiency of their cars. When a new home is built, the work is not over. A wise person will constantly maintain and update the home to make it better over time. It is vital that you never become complacent. You can always become smarter and stronger regardless of your age. When a sports team wins a championship, the improvement does not stop. They have to work harder than ever in the off season. Expectations become higher when you achieve great things.

Laser Focus

Your goals must always be the center of attention in your life. You have to eat, breath and sleep what you want to achieve. People may ridicule you for being obsessed with your goals, but that's a good thing. You don't want to be mediocre or normal. Normal people live paycheck to paycheck. Normal people only get 1 or 2 weeks of vacation a year. Normal people are overweight. Normal people are in debt. Normal people go to work every day on a job they dislike. High achievement calls for extraordinary action. Lewis Latimer and Thomas Edison, the light bulb and electricity men, spent extraordinary time in the Laboratory. Tiger Woods spent an extraordinary amount of time practicing his golf swing.

Write down your goals and be specific about what you want to achieve. Before the Empire State building was constructed, the builders had a specific architectural design to guide them on exactly what it should look like, the materials needed, and the construction timeline. You also need to construct your life with transcribed goals and plans to stay focused on exactly what you want. Your life is much more important than the Empire State building. If you want to save money, then write down a specific dollar amount. If you want to lose weight, then write down the exact amount.

Focus on one major goal at a time. Don't spread your energy too thin. I have seen very smart people run on the treadmill of achievement. They never gain traction because they don't stay persistent on one objective long enough. When one endeavor does not show immediate results, they bounce to another. It's like never giving a seed enough time to spread its roots. The masses never take the time to complete one objective before moving to another task.

Once you become an expert and successful at one thing, then you will have the resources and time to branch out. Hammer one nail at a time. When a tree grows, it forms one strong trunk before it begins to grow different branches and leaves. The most successful achievers and companies follow this course. Many businessmen try to launch multiple businesses at the same time. None of them ever gain traction because they do not focus on one long enough to see it prosper.

Google started with the focus of having the best search engine on the internet. After the company established itself as the best search engine, it got involved in smart phones, eyeglasses, home security, computer hardware, robotics, etc. General Electric's first main focus was electricity. General Electric is now involved in healthcare, aviation, finance, oil and gas, etc. The key is not to let external forces distract you. Most people do not achieve their chief aim because they get diverted from their path. Unwavering focus is the foundation of every great accomplishment.

Avoid Mass Media Distractions

Poor people have big Televisions. Rich people have big libraries. -Jim Rohn

Be careful how you spend your time. Everybody has the same 24 hours in a day. Rich people spend the majority of their hours on meaningful tasks that will enhance their lives. The masses spend the majority of their time watching television, playing games and engrossed in social media. Entertainment media distracts the masses from productive activities that sprout lasting achievement and long-term happiness. Your subconscious mind is like a sponge that will soak up whatever you feed it. Most of the programs on TV are based on negativity such as war, political bickering, crime, illness and poverty. Do not fill your mind with destructive content. You would not put low quality octane gas into a Ferrari, so why input negative low grade programming into your mind. What you feed your subconscious mind will manifest into your life. All forms of mass media should be kept to a minimal.

When you are pursuing your dreams, you do not have time to be a spectator in life. The athletes in the sports arena and the celebrities on the TV screen are already living their dreams. You need to stay busy making progress toward your goals. Don't waste time keeping up with sports statistics and celebrity gossip. The average person watches 5 to 7 hours of television per day. The typical person will spend approximately 17 years of his or her lifetime consuming mass media. Just imagine if you spent 17 years improving yourself and working on your goals. You would be able to achieve incredible feats. Respecting your time is a must. If you disrespect your time, then you are disrespecting your life. Time is a terrible thing to waste.

Read books instead of watching TV or playing on social media. Listen to personal finance lectures while you are cooking or cleaning. Listen to audio books when you are in the car. Turn driving time into learning time. Keep your mind sharp even if you already have a high level of achievement. Fortify your wisdom every day with a book. Even if you read the same book multiple times, you will always grasp something new. All of the wisdom you seek has already been written in a book. Wisdom is more important than money. When you are wise, the money will follow. The more you learn, the more you earn.

No Shortcuts to Success

When achievements are made quickly and easily, they usually become burdens in the long run. Building a $20 million business is a tedious and long process, but it is better than winning a $20 million lottery prize. In the long process of building a $20 million business, you will develop skills and business savvy. You can also teach your business skills to others. People would be willing to pay you for your consultation. Your knowledge would be in high demand and no one could ever take that from you. If Warren Buffet gave away all his money, he would easily become a billionaire all over again. He has a billionaire's mentality that can't be taken away. Wealth creation is similar to a kid learning how to ride a bike. It is a skill that you never lose once you master it. You will also have a greater appreciation for money when you have to work for it.

The typical person who is lucky enough to win the lottery is really not lucky at all. In the long run, a grand prize lottery ticket would become a burden for most people. There is no financial wisdom gained in winning the lottery. The majority of lottery winners end up broke a few years later. It is better to learn how to fish than for someone to give you fish. You will always be able to eat if you learn how to fish. There is no way to avoid the price you have to pay for anything that is worth having. There are no shortcuts to victory. This is why many professional athletes end up broke. They receive millions of dollars throughout their career, but never learn the science of money management, entrepreneurship and investing.

Many obese people try to take weight loss shortcuts through liposuction or trendy diet pills.

They lose weight fast in the beginning, but never learn about the science of nutrition and exercise which is needed to keep the weight off long term. They pay the price in the end by gaining all of their weight back. It's much better to lose the weight slowly by learning the principles of healthier eating and lifestyle change. If you want long lasting success in any endeavor, you have to earn it. Do not follow the masses who are always looking for the easy route. The true road to success is less crowded. There is less traffic in your way when you go the extra mile.

Surround Yourself with Winners

You cannot fly like an eagle if you consistently hang around turkeys. You must seek out others who are already successful and who are actively pursuing noteworthy goals. Iron sharpens iron. Ambitious people push each other to achieve greatness. You will grow if you are around people who are superior to you intellectually and financially. If you want to become stronger, then lift weights with people who are stronger than you.

The attitudes, ideas and work habits of other people will rub off on you, for better or for worse. You must eliminate all people from your life who are not conducive to your future progress. People are either for you or against you. Even neutral people are dangerous because they can become distractions. You can't grow if you are consistently surrounded by people who have a low level of ambition. It may temporarily boost your ego to feel superior to everyone in your circle, but you will not make any significant improvements in your life.

You will lose many friends as you become successful. Do not worry because they were only dead weight who could not keep up with your level of progress. You were born to be an Eagle, not a Duck. Eagles are apex predators who prefer flying alone. Ducks and other weaker species of birds like to flock in the comfort of large groups. When you climb higher on the ladder of success, it is less crowded and the air is fresher. You will have similar intelligence and income of the closest five people you associate with. You do not want to be the smartest person in your social circle. You should be around people who will challenge and uplift you.

If you befriend eight millionaires, sooner or later you will be the ninth millionaire of the group. It is crucial to be careful of the company you keep. If you let a person in your inner circle, make sure he or she is advancing in their life. Only allow quality people into your circle. If you are not currently surrounded by progressive people, then it is better to be alone. Sometimes you can make more gains if you walk the path alone. You will feel alone anyway if you are around people who are not on your same level of consciousness. Not only will you feel alone, you will also be dragged down by their negative spirit. The crab could easily get out of the bucket if he was in the bucket alone and did not have others pulling him down. Most people will always try to keep you from moving towards your highest potential. They are not inherently bad people; they just don't want you to leave. They will miss you. Misery loves company. They don't want to be forced to look in the mirror and wonder why they are not making similar progress in their lives.

In the beginning stages of progress, one must endure some degree of isolation. Do not worry for this lonely period will only be temporary. When people escape the mediocrity mindset, they will eventually meet other high achievers. Like-minded people will eventually find each other. There are several ways to immediately bring successful people into your circle. You can instantly pick the brain of world class achievers by reading the many books they have written. Another way is to go to conferences and seminars based on your field of interest. Network with progressive people who share similar ambitions.

CHAPTER 3

FINDING YOUR PURPOSE IN LIFE

There is no passion to be found playing small, in settling for a life that is less than the one you are capable of living. – Nelson Mandela

You were born on this earth for a reason. Life is the ultimate gift a person can receive. You have many great things to accomplish. Fulfilling your life's purpose is a never ending process. Having goals will separate you from the masses. Most people drift through life without setting any significant goals. They are comfortable with basic survival. You were not born to merely survive, you were born to thrive. Many adults had extraordinary goals when they were growing up as a child. They may have dreamed of becoming an actor, artist, politician, musician, astronaut, doctor, entrepreneur, etc. The masses allow society to beat their dreams out of them as they grow into adulthood. Only about 5 percent of the population will hold on to their childhood dreams and pursue them as adults. High achievers are mentally strong enough to ignore pessimism and distractions.

Do not conform to mediocre environmental influences and negative peer groups. The masses pursue mediocre goals if any at all. You can be different. Most people make ambiguous statements like "I want to be rich" or "I just want to be happy." They don't have a precise vision. If you have an unclear vision, then you will reap unclear results. Mediocre people drift throughout life, hoping to land at some fabulous destination. Drifting without a specific destination will get you nowhere fast. Successful people are not lucky. There is nothing lucky about setting a goal and consistently working toward its realization. You will not have an enjoyable life if you do not pursue a major life purpose. The most enjoyable times in life are when you are in pursuit of a major goal.

Without having a chief aim, a person is susceptible to a life of demise and depression. High achievers always create superior goals and never rest on their laurels. If you do not set a course for your life, external negative forces will lead you down a gloomy path of wretchedness. Many people get hung up on finding a single purpose in life. You can and should have more than one purpose. Life has different levels. As you reach higher levels in life, your goals will soon change. You will become a different person as you grow, therefore you will inevitably have new objectives.

Awaken Your Passion

Everyone is born with at least one talent. It is everyone's duty to develop and share their talent with the rest of the world. Your talent is established from what you naturally enjoy. You will never reach your peak potential if you don't enjoy your craft. If you don't enjoy what you do, then you won't be motivated to put the extra effort needed to develop your talents to maximum capacity. You should love what you do so much that you do not feel the difference between work and play. Maintaining consistency and focus is easy when you love your work. Adversity and mistakes will not deter you. No obstacle can stand in your way when you are passionate about your occupation. Your enthusiasm for your work will pull you through hard times and setbacks.

Yes, you can make a living and survive at doing something you don't love, but you will not excel to the highest levels if your heart is not in it. Life is all about progress and growing infinitely. The masses work at a job they don't like just to get by and survive. It's OK in the beginning, but in the long run, merely surviving is not enough. Work becomes depressing and mind numbing even when making a high income. In the long run, a great income will not satisfy you if you don't love what you do. The only way to live a life of fulfillment is to earn a living from what you enjoy doing. Consistent practice will develop your expertise. When you have expertise in any chosen endeavor, money will follow.

You will know when you have found your calling in life. It will feel natural and you will love working on it. Your calling is usually centered around something you naturally love doing. What would you like to do if money was not an issue? Pablo Picasso loved to paint, Warren Buffet loves to invest and Wolf Gang Puck loves to cook. Most people don't realize that they can do what they love and make a living or even a fortune doing it. Turn your passion into a business. You can build a brand or reputation and earn money from any passion you have.

I knew a college athlete who had a strong passion for the sport of football. He was a very talented player expected to play in the National Football League (NFL). Unfortunately, he suffered a career ending injury in his senior year. His injury prevented him from playing in the NFL. Nevertheless, he did not let his injury keep him from pursuing his passion for the sport of football. He decided to become a football coach. He started off coaching high school football and ten years later he eventually became an assistant coach in the NFL, where he earns over $500,000 per year. There is always more than one way you can make a living from what you enjoy. Disc Jockey Michiel Verwest, also known as DJ Tiesto, makes over $250,000 per night spinning records while people dance. He may not sing or play an instrument, but he still found a way to make a fortune from his passion for music.

Allocate some time every day to building your dream. Even if you are currently working a full-time job, you can still work on your dream part-time. The busier you are, the more you will accomplish. A busy person will accomplish more because he or she does not take time for granted. Every hour of the day is maximized. Time will fly when you are obsessed with bringing your dream to fruition. When you are working on something you love, you do not know the difference between work and play. Life is meant to be enjoyed. If you are working just for the money, then your soul will not be fulfilled. You should not need an alarm clock to wake up in the morning. Your ambition and love for your trade should wake you up. Moderate your partying and other social activities. You should often say no when friends invite you out for weekend festivities. Magnificent rewards await those who delay gratification. Do the work you have to do now, so tomorrow you can have a privileged lifestyle.

Billionaire Daniel Snyder is the majority owner of the Washington Redskins. He made his first million when he was about 20 years old. Instead of focusing on partying during his college years, he chose to focus on wealth building. He dropped out of college to run a business out of his parent's house.

His company leased jets to fly college students to spring break in Ft. Lauderdale and the Caribbean. He capitalized on everyone else's need to party. While everybody else was partying, he was quietly building a fortune. Business comes first. Put in the extra work that others are not willing to do. People will call your compulsive work ethic weird, but when you become prosperous they will call you a genius. When your major purpose becomes an obsession you will be unstoppable. External forces and adversity won't stand a chance at holding you back. Progress will be slow at first, but momentum will build similar to how a snowball rolls down a mountainside and grows into a powerful avalanche.

Monetize Your Passion Online

Your major purpose in life should also be connected to serving others. The more people you serve, the more enhanced your life will be. The internet allows you to impact an unlimited amount of people. When your major purpose is based on service to others, you will have unlimited rewards. You should impact as many people's lives as you can with your passion. Everything you thought was just a hobby or passion can be monetized to create a living for yourself via the internet. The internet is the great equalizer. Nobody can stop you from serving the world with your talent. Industries that were once difficult to break into are now easily accessible if you are dedicated and determined.

Before the internet, personal trainers could only serve a small number of clients in a gym. Servicing a small amount of people limited their income. The internet now allows personal trainers to become millionaires by teaching and inspiring millions of people. Personal trainers impact millions by selling workout videos, vitamins, fitness gear and diet plans online. Technology has made reaching and servicing the world easier than ever.

The internet offers unlimited money making possibilities because new people come online every day. There is unlimited earning potential. Every new person online is a potential new client or subscriber to your product or service. Millions of people in the world who share your interest and passion are waiting to connect with you. Only half of the world is currently connected online. The internet will continue to have massive growth in the future.

The money will come if you are dedicated and consistent. There is a guitar teacher who profits well from his passion for music. He never became a rock star or even had his own band. He took his knowledge of guitar playing and made tutorial videos on the internet. Millions of guitar students click on his videos and pay a small monthly fee to watch and learn. He is now able to make a great living from his passion for playing the guitar. His website allows him to have an unlimited amount of guitar students. A soccer mom earns $70,000 a month online from selling her handmade headbands and socks. Nigerian entrepreneur Chinedu Echeruo sold his mobile navigation app to Apple for $1 billion. Opportunities to earn money online are limitless. It is possible for you to monetize whatever you love.

Expect to Win

Expect your dreams to come true. It is imperative that you keep an optimistic state of mind when pursuing your purpose in life. Plug into optimistic sources of energy every day. Sources of encouragement are goals you have written down; motivational audios; personal development books; and fraternizing with successful people. No matter what adversity you encounter, circumstances will improve as long as you keep pushing forward. No matter how cold or harsh winter can be, a sunny spring has never failed to follow. You must believe your endeavors will be successful. A positive attitude is a magnet for good fortune. Train your mind to look for the good in everything.

Your attitude will determine the heights of your

achievements. The universe will reward those who are grateful. This is similar to a parent who gives a child a gift. When the child is appreciative and grateful for what has been given, the parent is more inspired to reward the child again. Life is the same way. Display your appreciation and you will be showered with more blessings.

Have gratitude while continuing to strive for more at the same time. Never lose perspective on how far you have already come, while keeping the vision of where you want to go. Every day is a clean slate when you wake up healthy with a sound mind and body. Every day is a blessing and another opportunity to move closer to your goals. There are a lot of people in the world who would love to be in your shoes. Don't take this day for granted, but take it with gratitude.

CHAPTER 4
THE KEYS TO FINANCIAL FREEDOM

Life is a game; money is how we keep score. - Ted Turner

Becoming wealthy should be one of your major goals in life. Wealth equals freedom. Throughout history, people have understood that freedom is the embodiment of life. Freedom is so important that people have fought wars and died for it. In developed nations, most people have freedom of speech; freedom to vote; freedom of religion, etc. One of the most important freedoms that continues to elude the masses is financial freedom. When you have financial freedom you own all of your time. Time is arguably your most valuable asset. Once time is gone you can never replenish it. Time is a priceless resource. The working masses have limited time to do what they desire and be around the people they love. When you are a typical employee, sometimes you have to miss a child's sporting event, school recital, birthday party, friend's barbeque, etc. Those are special moments that you can never get back. A person with financial freedom has unlimited time to partake in all of the pleasures of life. The average employee only has one or two weeks of vacation per year. This is not a balanced lifestyle. It can be somewhat depressing when it is time to report back to work after a one-week or two-week vacation. When you are on vacation, it takes at least 4 days to get adjusted to your new environment. By the second week when you are finally in the groove and enjoying yourself, it's time to go back home. One cannot really explore, absorb, and become totally refreshed with a meager two-week vacation. When you are wealthy you have the time and resources to turn your life into a never ending holiday.

A middle class Dad makes plans to go see his daughter's soccer game after work. When he is ready to leave work, his boss tells him he must stay for several hours of mandatory overtime. He feels pressured to stay because his job is his only source of income and he is afraid to disappoint his boss. Meanwhile, his daughter is sad when she does not see her Dad on the sidelines at the game. Dad should have the freedom to be in attendance at each of her soccer games. The rich do what they want and the masses do what they are told. Having the freedom to spend more time with family or to take as much vacation as you need should be all the motivation you need to become wealthy. Your freedom is the most important asset money can buy.

Working to become an elite wealth builder will ultimately allow you to live life on your own terms.

Having wealth will also afford you unlimited time to pursue the type of work you passionate about. Most people have to work on jobs they don't enjoy. Millions of people are forced to work jobs they dislike and associate with people they abhor for 30 to 40 years. Approximately 70 percent of employees are disengaged and uninspired at work, according to Gallup's 2013 State of the American Workplace Report. This is modern day bondage with invisible chains. The transparent chains consist of 30 year mortgages, car payments and general debt based consumerism.

The good news is that anyone can make a change. You can have complete freedom and live a limitless life if you decide to build wealth. Becoming wealthy is a choice. This is a decision that most people never make. You are not meant to conform and live a mediocre lifestyle. You are a limitless individual intended for greatness.

The Millionaire Mindset

Why do the rich become richer and the poor become poorer? There are many socioeconomic reasons for this, but the number one reason people remain poor is their mindset. Over 80 percent of millionaires are first generation self-made. They did not inherit their wealth. The majority of millionaires were once poor or middle class like the masses. Elite wealth builders are humans just like everyone else. They have to sleep, eat and breath like everyone else. The thing that makes them different is their mentality. They decided to adopt the mindset of abundance instead of scarcity. They decided that mediocrity was unacceptable.

Self-made millionaires decided to think differently than the masses. At the end of the week, common people say, "Thank God it's Friday," because they can't wait to escape their unrewarding jobs. World class people look forward to their work because they enjoy the challenge of pursuing their dreams. Warren Buffet loves investing in stocks and analyzing the markets. I'm sure he looks forward to Mondays so he can get back to work on his passion. The wealthy have a lot of free time to work on their personal dreams. The masses are discontent because they are being paid to work on someone else's dream. It is hard to have relentless passion when you are working on someone else's vision.

The poor and middle classes enjoy talking about winning the lottery; buying new cars; bigger homes; and general spending. The lottery is a tax on the poor and 99 percent will never win anyway. Hyper consumerism only traps people with debt. You should be encircled with people who discuss investments, business ideas, and general wealth building. Instead of discussing ideas on how to waste money, you need to brainstorm with others about accumulating assets that rise in value such as dividend paying stocks, real estate, precious metals, etc. If you consistently purchase income producing assets, you will eventually become rich. If you are always purchasing liabilities, you never become financially free.

Saving, investing and business ownership is how wealth is created. It is easy to see why the rich get richer and the poor get poorer. What kind of conversations are you having? You will become what you talk and think about most of the time. Your purpose and impact on the world is only limited by your imagination and desire for greatness. Do not conform to another person's lack of vision and imagination. If you don't work on your own plans, then you will always have to work under someone else's plans. Society will not have great plans for you. Create your own destiny, dream big and take massive action.

You are going to end up somewhere in life regardless, so you may as well aim for a fabulous destination. If you board a sailboat and want to arrive at a beautiful island like Maui, then you need to specifically aim for that destination. If you go drifting without a sail and a compass, then you could arrive in the middle of a hurricane. If you focus your mind in the direction of financial freedom, then you will surely get there. If you are not motivated to attain financial freedom, then you will always have to work for a paycheck, which will consequently keep your life in check. To live life to the fullest, you will need abundance. There is simply no way around it. Wealth will give you options in life. You are meant to have the best. Affluent people have the option of choosing the best of everything. They can enjoy the finest health care, neighborhoods, education, vacations, etc. Never believe in the myth that rich people are greedy or evil. Money is not the root of all evil. Having money is not evil. Money is a neutral tool. A person could use $500 to buy food and feed the poor or to buy a stolen gun and harm someone. Money does not change people; it only makes them more of who they already are. If you are a virtuous person, then money will help you spread more joy to the world. If you are wicked, then money can help you spread more turmoil. A righteous person can spread more happiness in the world with money than he or she can without it.

Global Wealth

The average person in a developed country has a better standard of living than any King or Queen during medieval times. Developed nations are so abundant that anybody who is industrious and dedicated can become rich over time. If you live in an industrialized nation, you should gratefully take advantage of opportunities and tools at your disposal to become affluent. Attaining wealth is a very realistic goal. You received the lucky roll of the dice if you were born into a first world economy. Billionaire Investor Warren Buffet attributes a lot of his financial success to being born in a developed nation.

Many immigrants become very prosperous when they migrate to developed nations. They do not squander their chance to participate and prosper in a functioning economy. You should adopt the mindset and determination of an immigrant. The typical immigrant does not take opportunities for granted.

There are no excuses for financial lack if you are able to work and conduct business in an industrialized region of the world. The internet has opened up the doors of prosperity even wider. Technology has created a new Golden age of prosperity. Never before in history have so many individuals obtained millionaire status at such a young age. The number of millionaires in America actually increased after the great recession of 2008. Many people have moved up and joined the ranks of the wealthy. There are over 12 million people worldwide who each have a net worth of more than a million dollars. The number of millionaires will continue to grow. If you are determined and focus, your financial future will also be bright. You can be one of the next millionaires.

Set Specific Financial Goals

Be specific about how much money you want. Uncertain goals attract vague results. It is not good enough to just say you want to be rich. When you go to a restaurant, you order exactly what you want to eat from the menu. You should also be precise when setting financial goals.

What is the exact dollar amount you need to live the lifestyle you want? An ideal long term financial goal is to have a large sum of money, which you can live off the interest and never have to spend the principle. Write down your thirty-year long-term financial goal somewhere you can see it every day. Also, write down your five year and ten year financial objectives. A dream is not a goal until you write it down. Thinking big is great, but it can be beneficial to set smaller goals and work your way up. Smaller goals allow you to document progress more rapidly. You will reach your major goal quicker if you set smaller attainable objectives. Small incremental gains will add up to a huge victory. Don't get discouraged if you don't meet certain deadlines. As long as you are moving the ball forward, you will eventually hit your mark.

If you desire to become a millionaire, then first set the goal of having $10,000. Once you have $10,000, reaching $25,000 will feel believable.

Once you have $25,000, then having $50,000 will feel very achievable. Before you know it, you will have $100,000. After you have $100,000 in the bank, becoming a millionaire will not seem like a difficult task. After you have your first $1,000,000, you can realistically aim for $5,000,000 or more! You will begin to fraternize with elite achievers and industry leaders. The high expectations of your new social circle will rub off on you.

Financial freedom is all about having options and independence. Luxurious living is a secondary benefit. Your goal should be to experience everything life has to offer without having to stress about money. Why would you settle for less? Becoming rich is possible, but not easy. Nothing worth having in life is accomplished easily. It is better to exert the effort needed to become affluent than to settle for being middle class or impoverished. There is no easy route in life. The challenges of living in poverty far outweigh the adversity of becoming rich. It is wiser to choose the path to prosperity.

If you currently earn $50,000 a year, then you can eventually earn $50,000 a month. This may sound unrealistic to the average person, but you should not think like the average person. You should think like the elite. Imagine if you had dinner with Warren Buffet or Bill Gates. If you told them your goal was to make $50,000 a month, they would probably smile and say, "that's all you want?" They would think your financial goal is too low. They would encourage you to aim higher. Michelangelo said, "The greater danger for most of us lies not in setting our aim too high and falling short, but in setting our aim too low, and achieving our mark."

Your first time at anything will usually be a challenge. The first time you learned how to walk was a challenge. The first time you learned to ride a bike was a challenge. Now, you can walk and ride very easily. Making your first $1,000,000 will be the most challenging. Every $1,000,000 you make after the first will become easier. Over time, you will become better at recognizing wealth building opportunities. A financial guru is created from experience and repetition. The wisdom you will have gained once you make your first million is priceless. No one can ever take your knowledge from you. You will never lose your wealthy state of mind.

Save Your Money

If you cannot save money, the seeds of greatness are not in you. - W. Clement Stone

The person who doesn't know where his next dollar is coming from usually doesn't know where his last dollar went. - Unknown

You should always pay yourself first. Save all the money you can. Many financial gurus recommend you save 10 percent of your income. I think you should save at least 30 percent of your net income. You must be a radical saver if you want to achieve financial freedom at a rapid pace. It is very possible to save more than 30 percent of your income if you adopt a frugal lifestyle. There are many super savers who save more than 50 percent of their income.

No matter how much you earn, you will never have financial peace if you do not learn how to save. Saving should be an unconscious habit like eating and sleeping. The more money you accumulate; the more peace of mind you will have. With every dollar you save, you are getting one step closer to financial freedom. It is best to have your savings automated. Your savings should automatically go into an account that is not easy for you to withdraw. It is best not to have a Debit/ATM card attached to this account. Therefore, you will not be tempted to dip into your savings because it will not be easily available to withdraw. Keep a separate checking account for monthly bills and daily expenses. When you save your money, you are treating it well. Money loves attention. When you treat your friends well, they will introduce you to their friends and you will have more connections. When you treat money well, it will invite more money into your life. Any person or thing you treat well will reciprocate.

Saving money alone will not make you rich, but it does set a solid foundation. Not only should you save your money, but you should also invest your money and let it grow. Magnificent investment opportunities always come like a gift when you least expect it. The masses almost never have extra savings available to take advantage of these gifts. The great recession of 2008-2009 was the opportunity of a lifetime for anyone with extra savings to invest. Shares in great Fortune 500 companies could have been bought at fire sale prices. Many homes throughout America could have been purchased for less than $10,000. Diligent savers and investors were having a field day with the array of economic opportunities.

Having money attracts more money. When you have saved and displayed financial prudence, banks and private investors are more likely to invest in your ideas. Many people also have become wealthy by using their own savings to fund personal business ideas. Business woman, Sara Blakely used $5,000 in personal savings to fund her women's undergarment company. Sara Blakely eventually became a Billionaire. Her savings gave her business the capital it needed. There is no downfall to saving. Once you have an extraordinary amount of money, you will be a magnet for privileged opportunities. Money will begin to work for you instead of you working for money.

Live Below Your Means

People who fake it until they make it are never going to make it. The masses go into debt purchasing luxury goods they don't need in an attempt to appear successful. Luxurious living should be enjoyed only after you can truly afford it. Babies learn to crawl before they walk. A child uses training wheels to learn how to ride a bike. Do not adopt grandiose spending habits that will impede you from building wealth. There are many people who have high annual incomes, but still live one paycheck away from disaster. The money you are able to save and invest is more important than the high wages you earn. People who pretend to be rich typically use borrowed money to purchase luxury homes, cars, boats, jewelry and clothes.

The majority of people who live lavishly are not wealthy. They appear to have a high standard of living, but in reality have a low quality of life because of debt. The things they purchase actually own them. In spite of their high salaries, they have a relatively low net worth. Pretenders do not have peace of mind. An abundance of unnecessary material possessions will weigh you down, distract you, and prevent wealth accumulation. Always live below your means. Even rich people continue to live below their means if they want to stay rich.

Living below their means is how they became wealthy. Bill Gates is one of the richest people in the world and he does not own a yacht. He can surely afford one, but he only rents a yacht when needed. Why bother with the headache of ownership? Owning a yacht means he would have to pay for maintenance, docking fees, and a host of other miscellaneous expenses. It is always better to rent depreciating luxury items.

In pursuit of your financial fortune, beware of the pitfalls of purchasing liabilities. Use your money to purchase income producing assets. It is difficult to focus on building wealth if you tax yourself with an abundance of material objects that require a lot of maintenance. You will progress into having unlimited wealth if you don't swamp yourself with hyper consumption. As you start your journey towards financial freedom, you need to live as light as possible. Buying the best quality is smart, but paying double or triple the price for something only because of luxury name brand status will keep you poor. Buying the best quality does not necessarily mean it has to be the most expensive. Spending a little more for quality can save you money in the long run from having to replace inferior goods. The best quality is normally in the middle price range, which is not cheap, but not outrageously expensive either. This is especially true with automobiles and clothing. Corporations profit on the low self-esteem of people who feel that purchasing the most expensive brand will give them higher socioeconomic status.

Luxury brand marketers key in on people with average incomes aspiring to look wealthy without actually being wealthy. It is easier to wear and drive symbols of wealth before putting in the risk, hard work and sacrifice needed to obtain it. You should never concern yourself with purchasing luxury goods until after you become a high net worth individual.

Going into debt for an automobile is one of the major reasons the masses cannot accumulate wealth. If you can't pay cash, then you can't afford it. Approximately 80 percent of cars on the road are financed through a loan or a lease. Those monthly car payments could be saved and invested. With the proliferation of online transportation apps and ride share programs, it has become easier than ever to function without owning a vehicle. If you are going to finance a vehicle, then it should be an inexpensive model that you can afford to pay off in less than 2 years. Most cars will last you 20 years or more with proper maintenance.

The auto industry encourages people to buy a new car every three years to keep up with the coolest trends and maintain their social status. This is a losing game for working class people. A car is nothing but a mode of transportation. The only reason a person needs a car is to get from point (A) to point (B). Being a stop light celebrity is not worth going into debt. The truth is, no one will really care about your fancy car and it will usually attract attention from the wrong crowd.

Presenting a true impression to the world is not done with material goods. A true impression is exhibited with the content of your character and the lifestyle you live. When you are truly wealthy, you will vibrate a special energy, which will gravitate people to you. World class people display wealth with the freedom they have. They can play golf in the middle of the day; wake up whenever they feel like it; and take a vacation at a moment's notice. A sophisticated demeanor will define you more than any luxury brand ever could. When you become limitless, your lifestyle is your brand.

Celebrities on TV flaunting luxurious items and living in mega mansions are good for TV ratings, but that is not how most millionaires live. You would not recognize the typical millionaire if you saw one. The majority of rich people drive cars and wear clothes that are low key and unassuming. They fly under the radar. Most people with massive wealth don't feel the need to purchase extravagant symbols of success. If you want luxury items, then invest in income producing assets that will pay for them. Intelligent wealth builders use passive income from rental properties, dividends or capital gains to pay for luxury items. Effortless income should pay for extravagant goods. One should never indulge in opulence with borrowed money or income earned from working on a job.

Dump Your Debt

The borrower is slave to the lender – Proverbs 22:7

Going into debt is a sign of someone who lacks the ability to delay gratification. Most people don't have the patience to save money to pay cash for the consumer goods they desire. Do not spend money before you actually have the money! It is very easy for credit card spending to spiral out of control. One unnecessary purchase usually leads to another. A person might buy a new suit and then he or she will want new shoes to match. A person will want a big screen TV and then new furniture. Many people say spending with credit feels like free money because there is no emotional attachment to the transaction. Credit card debt will stifle financial growth and disturb your peace of mind. It is always best to pay with cash. You will spend less when you pay with cash. It is easy to swipe a card, but difficult to part with cash in your pocket. Having cash on hand is empowering and you are less likely to make senseless impulse purchases. Credit cards are only useful when paying for airline tickets, hotels, car rentals, online purchases, etc. Do not use a credit card unless you have enough cash readily available to pay off the balance in full by the end of the month.

Practice delaying your purchases. If you delay a purchase, you will usually forget about it because it probably was not a significant need. The majority of personal credit card debt comes from impulse purchases that are not necessities of life. Let's face it, most people impulse shop because they are bored. Many people use shopping as entertainment and consume beyond their means in order to fulfill an emotional void. Do not go into debt purchasing material goods in an attempt to impress friends and strangers. They are not going to pay your bill. Credit card abuse will only give you a temporary high followed by a huge let down when the bill comes due. Shopping should not be used for entertainment. Shopping is not a hobby! Find a hobby that will not put you into financial ruin such as gardening, cycling, sewing, painting, reading, chess, surfing, etc. This is why having goals are so important. If you are working towards your goals, you won't have time to indulge in hyper-consumerism. The people you see camping out in front of the mall during holiday sales have too much time on their hands.

Credit is a tool that can be beneficial if used properly, but dangerous if used irresponsibly. Credit has an influence on just about everything in our modern society. Your credit score will have a great impact on your life. This is why you must learn to use credit sensibly. If you do not responsibly pay back creditors, then society will not believe you are trustworthy in other aspects of life. A poor credit score will make it very difficult for you to lease an apartment, buy a home, purchase a car, find gainful employment, etc.

The abuse of credit will enslave you for the rest of your life if you don't manage it well. Many people must work overtime or two jobs just to pay creditors. The money you make will not be yours to keep if you are deep in debt. You will not be able to enjoy the items you purchased with debt because you will be too busy working to pay off the bills. You cannot spend your free time and energy working for creditors and simultaneously work toward your major purpose in life. It is impossible to serve two masters.

America is a culture that loves instant gratification. Nothing valuable will come quick and easy. Nothing in life is free. It is always best to pay upfront rather than pay later with interest. After three or four months of making loan payments, material goods begin to lose their luster anyway. Don't become a slave to debt.

Renting vs. Buying a Home

The word mortgage means "Death Pledge" in Latin.

Just because you can afford the monthly payments on a home does not necessarily mean you should buy one. When you calculate 30 years of mortgage interest, property taxes, home insurance, maintenance, utilities, furniture, etc., you will end up paying a lot more than what you expected. Home ownership is overrated as an investment. I am not a big advocate of people having the majority of their money and time locked into a single family home.

Home ownership will take a toll on your free time that could be used to work on your life's purpose. Most of your weekends will be spent shopping at hardware stores, remodeling, cleaning, repairing and lawn mowing. There is always something to improve or maintain on a house even if it's brand new. You are like a free handy man for the mortgage lender who is the real property owner.

A single family home is more of a liability than it is an asset. There is no guarantee a house will rise high in value. Even when a home does rise in value, annual expenses for repairs, renovations, remodeling, taxes and insurance will usually negate typical home appreciation rates. Purchasing a home does not automatically make sense for families either. A family can find numerous spacious homes available for rent. Home ownership was a beacon of success during the old manufacturing economy. It was the American Dream and meant that you had made it to the good life. This is no longer the case.

Home ownership no longer signifies how successful you are. There are many millionaires who prefer to rent instead of owning. These people already know they are rich; hence, they don't need to actually own a house to prove their success. Many of the super-rich elect the maintenance free lifestyle of renting.

Whether or not you should buy a home depends on your personal situation. People have different circumstances and real estate markets vary from city to city. Make sure you do your research; consider all options; and don't rush into it. It is ok to rent a residence until you have done your due diligence and are sure where you want to live long-term. Owning a single family home can be a wonderful experience, but it is not suited for everyone.

If you are young or single, then you should always lean towards renting and stay as mobile as possible. A mortgaged home will weigh you down. You never know when you'll want to pursue more profitable economic opportunities in another state or country. Most young people are usually not well traveled enough to know which city in the world is best suited for them. It would be wise to do a lot of traveling before you consider planting roots in one location through home ownership. A single family home is not very liquid, so you cannot always sell it quickly when you are ready to leave.

This is not the old economy when it was normal

for a person to find a job and work in the same city for 30 or 40 years. We are in a worldwide mobile economy. You will have more opportunities if you are mobile. Even if you prefer to work with one organization, you will move up the career ladder faster if you are mobile and willing to move. Many people have enjoyed a lot of career success simply because their mobility allowed them to seize opportunities in other locations.

If you are absolutely certain you want to buy a home, then choose a desirable location and buy a house that is priced well below your affordability. Purchase a home you can afford to pay off in 10 years or less. Never embrace long-term personal debt. Less is best when it comes to home ownership. The smaller the home, the more money you will save on maintenance, property taxes and utilities. Buying a gigantic home with extra space you don't need will become a burden in the long run. The typical family does not need a 4500 square foot mini-mansion. The most important thing is to live in a safe and prosperous community.

Generating Income From Real Estate

There are many ways to profit from real estate without actually purchasing property. The conventional way most people invest in real estate is through purchasing and renting out multi-unit homes or apartment buildings. Using this approach will take a lot of experience, connections and energy to acquire income producing properties in desirable locations.

Real estate is all about location. The majority of desirable income producing real estate is located in thriving downtowns or near college campuses. Most of these properties are already owned by major corporations. If you are fortunate enough to find one available, it will usually command an extraordinarily high price that a beginner investor usually cannot afford. One would need a lot of cash or go into heavy debt in order to break into one of those markets. Being a landlord isn't always profitable either. It can sometimes be difficult to garner rent that provides enough money to cover mortgage payments, maintenance fees and property taxes. These expenses sometimes make it difficult to produce a profit at the end of the month.

One of the easiest ways to generate passive income from real estate is to purchase shares in a Real Estate Investment Trust (REIT). A REIT is a company that owns and sometimes operates income-producing real estate. REITs own many types of commercial real estate. These properties include office buildings, apartment buildings, warehouses, hospitals, shopping centers, hotels and even timberlands. The shares of many REITs are freely traded on a major stock exchange. REITs pay investors on a monthly or quarterly basis. Investors can also make gains when the company's share price rises in value. Investing in a REIT is a great way to receive effortless real estate income without the aggravations that come with being a landlord. Consistently buying more shares will eventually compensate an investor with a massive amount of reliable income.

The Truth About College

College can be beneficial, but it is not designed to teach you how to become wealthy. College teaches you how to assimilate into the marketplace as an employee. The typical college educated employee will usually get paid just enough to maintain a decent living, but not enough to become financially independent. A typical employee will usually work for 40 years or more. When the servitude is over, hopefully the employee has enough money saved and sufficient health to enjoy his or her senior years. Sadly, the majority of workers will not have sufficient money to enjoy their senior years with dignity and financial peace. The only thing most workers will have to show for their years of labor is a wooden plaque or a brass pin.

I am a big advocate of higher learning, but pursuing a degree in just any program will not guarantee you a high income. If you want to attend college, you have to be very careful about the type of degree you pursue. Make sure you choose a major that has value in the marketplace. College degrees associated with the Law, Finance, Accounting, Healthcare, Science, Engineering, or Information Technology are usually the best ones to pursue. If your passion is not associated with one of the aforementioned professions, then going to a trade school or getting real world entrepreneurial experience is all you need to start earning money. There are many college degrees that will definitely not guarantee you a respectable income. Some examples of college majors to be wary about are History, Art, Music, Theatre, English Literature, and Sports Management. You can study History or Music at home during your free time. Do not go into debt for degrees that will not facilitate a high income after graduation. Many people who obtain degrees without a high demand in the market place end up working unskilled jobs in the service sector. You can find a lot of college graduates working as waiters, bartenders, security guards, retail sales clerks, etc. Those are jobs they could have obtained without going to college. Education is very important, but you don't always have to enroll in a 4-year traditional university to learn a valuable skill. With sufficient training, you can become a Computer Programmer, Airplane Pilot, Carpenter, Paramedic, Sales Professional, Fireman, Policeman,

Plumber, Electrician, Aircraft Mechanic, Auto Mechanic, Gourmet Chef, Realtor, etc. Some of the most accomplished and wealthiest people in the world did not graduate high school or college. Notable high school or college dropouts consist of Bill Gates, Mark Zuckerberg, Steve Jobs, Brad Pitt, Ralph Lauren and Walt Disney to name a few. This is not to say everyone should drop out of high school or skip college. If you decide to enroll in college, make sure your major is in a subject that will propel you to realize your chief aim in life.

The Safe Job Fairy Tale

It is risky to rely on a job as your sole source of income. There is no such thing as a completely secure job. Anything can happen at any moment to turn your dream job into a nightmare. Poor management, mergers, automation, budget cuts, difficult co-workers and office politics can often disrupt many careers. An employee has many external factors which are out of his or her control. Employees are very vulnerable; no matter how educated or productive they are.

There is nothing wrong with working on a job if you enjoy it, but never depend on a job as your only source of cash flow. It is not wise to allow one institution or corporation to have total control over your financial future. I have seen smart people give all of their loyalty and talents to corporations for 20 or more years; but they were left with nothing after the company decided to move overseas for cheaper labor to cut expenses. Stockholders are more important to a business than employees. Most employees are seen as expendable resources. Corporations will never be 100 percent loyal to workers. It is nothing personal. It is just business and you have to see yourself as a business also. Treat your life like a business.

Do not believe in the middle class illusion. The typical middle class worker is only two paychecks away from poverty. The middle class lifestyle looks good on the surface because of the new cars and picturesque suburban homes. The cars and the homes are usually obtained through debt. Debt destroys freedom. They are obligated to work at monotonous jobs with people they don't like just to keep up with their middle class image.

Weekends consist of home maintenance chores and recreational shopping which puts them even deeper in debt. The lucky few might get a two-week annual vacation. The middle class continues to shrink every year. You must decide if you are going to be a part of the wealthy class or the poor class. Choose to be rich. No one can afford to aim for economic mediocrity anymore. If you want limitless wealth and freedom, then you must have the mentality of a business person. Working on a job should be viewed as a stepping stone and not the ultimate goal. The majority of companies pay workers just enough money so they won't quit, but not nearly enough money to become independently wealthy.

Even most entertainers and athletes are just glorified well paid employees. Many celebrities do not have the freedom to take a six-month vacation to travel the world. Most professional athletes and entertainers have nonstop year around obligations. They always have to be cautious about what they say, wear and do. One wrong statement or incident could put their careers in jeopardy. No matter how much money you earn, you will never have a financial security unless you create multiple streams of income. You cannot become complacent, even if you currently have a high income job you enjoy.

Workplace circumstances can always change. Therefore, it is important not to weigh yourself down with credit card debt, luxury cars and mortgages. At least 30 percent of your earnings from a job should be invested in appreciating assets or entrepreneurial endeavors. Don't be a spectator in life. Get in the game and impact the world. Create your own legacy. A noble person should be able to pass wealth to his or her great grandchildren. You cannot pass down your annual salary from a job to family or charity when you die.

Working hard at a job can make you a decent living, but working hard at becoming a great investor or entrepreneur can make you wealthy. Sometimes a high paying job is not advantageous. A high paying job gives some people a false sense of security. A large consistent paycheck encourages many people to stop learning, exploring and growing. People can lose their creativity, imagination and hunger for personal achievement outside of their employment. Many settle into a routine of working, eating junk food, watching TV and debt based spending. This monotonous lifestyle feels normal because all of their peers live the same way. Don't let a high paying job smother your creative passion. Even if you are a well paid employee, you must always stay hungry.

Many employees also become complacent once they receive an elaborate job title or work for a corporation with a prominent brand. Their job title or company's brand becomes their personal identity. You should never let a job define who you are. The promise of future advancement, medical benefits and a pension also help to extinguish a person's entrepreneurial flame. It's very risky to put all of your faith in corporate career promises.

The money you earn will usually hit a glass ceiling when you are an employee. Think outside the box when it comes to building wealth. Anyone with an entrepreneurial spirit can utilize the skills they've acquired on a job to start their own business. A truck driver could start his or her own transportation company. A policeman could start a security company or a private investigation firm. Many entrepreneurs started off working for someone else, which gave them knowledge and confidence to venture out and create their own enterprise. Billionaire entrepreneur Sachin Basal used to work as a software engineer for Amazon. He eventually co-founded a similar e-commerce company called Flipkart. Sachin Basal and his business partner Binny Bansal launched Flipkart from an apartment with a $6,500 investment.

World renown Chef Wolf Gang Puck could have easily continued working in the confines of a restaurant making an average living. He decided to use the culinary skills he learned as an employee to make a bigger impact on the world. Wolf Gang Puck impacted millions with cookbooks, cookware, appliances, TV appearances, and owning several restaurants. Chef Wolf Gang Puck amassed a net worth of over $75 million because he became an entrepreneur and did not allow anyone to put limits on his ideas and dreams. The bottom line is, if you want limitless wealth, freedom and creativity, you will have to diversify your income beyond a normal job.

Build Multiple Sources of Income

Wealthy people have many sources of income. A typical millionaire has approximately seven streams of income. The ideal way to live is to have multiple streams of income that will continue to flow even after the work is completed. Passive income is money received on a regular basis, with little effort required to maintain it. Monthly or quarterly dividends from stock ownership is one example of passive income. Intelligent wealth builders don't have to physically work hard every day for their money. Your money should work for you. Working hard on a job for the rest of your life is the worst way to make money. Your earnings will be limited on a typical job because you are trading time for money.

The majority of your discretionary income should be invested in assets that will produce revenue while you are sleeping. Savings from a job should be transferred to assets that will generate passive income. Owning a small apartment building or shares in a real estate investment trust (REIT) that garners $10,000 a month is better than earning $20,000 a month as a corporate employee. The apartment building owner or REIT shareholder can receive passive income while spending the whole winter on a tropical island. He or she could also use his or her free time to create more streams of income. The corporate employee still has to physically show up to work every day. There is also an elevated sense of gratification when you earn money from an investment you discovered or a business you created. Receiving a $500 check from royalties, rental income or dividend payments is more powerful than earning $1000 from overtime on a job. The way you make your money is more important than the amount.

Less is More

Your life should not be defined by your material possessions. The public storage industry in America makes over $20 billion in annual revenue. The storage industry makes billions off the masses who stockpile possessions they don't need or use. Too many people are slaves to materialism. This trend is quite disturbing. Real abundance comes from having unlimited time and freedom. Merely having a lot of things can stifle your pursuit of true happiness.

There is a popular author named Joshua Becker who writes about minimalism. He tells a story about when he spent a Saturday cleaning his cluttered garage. His son was in the back yard playing alone and wanted his dad to come join him. He felt unhappy because he was missing out on precious family time with his child. If it was not for all of the clutter that accumulated in the garage, he would have had time to play catch with his son. This was a turning point in his life and he decided to become a minimalist. He realized that the things he owned and barely ever used actually owned him. He sold and gave away the majority of his possessions. Afterwards, he felt wealthier because of the extra time he could spend with his family. He had less possessions to maintain and worry about, which made his life happier. A minimalist lifestyle helped him to obtain more freedom and peace of mind. Keep your life as simple as possible. Practicing minimalism can help you stay focused on what is really important.

Givers Always Gain

Money can afford you the finer aspects of life, but most importantly, it can help you become a better person. The more money you have; the more people you can help in the world. You could help end world hunger; fight for animal rights; combat homelessness, etc. Having wealth can strengthen the impact you make on whatever charity or movement you believe in. Oprah Winfrey built a school in Africa for girls. It would have been very difficult to construct a school for young girls had Oprah been poor.

Philanthropy can also give your life more meaning and a sense of fulfillment. There are many stories of wealthy celebrities who are suicidal and drug addicted. This is partly because they do not have a purpose greater than themselves. They lost their meaning in life. If your mind is idle without a purpose bigger than yourself, your mental wellbeing will take a turn for the worst. Using wealth to only enhance your own life has a point of diminishing returns. Material luxuries will eventually lose their sparkle. You will become dormant and dissatisfied with life. When water is stagnant, it becomes murky and impure. When it flows, it stays fresh and clean. Allow your money to flow and impact others.

The wealthiest people in the world are very generous with their money. They understand the laws of nature. Being generous to others will also bring you good fortune in return. You reap what you sow. When you open your hand to give you are also opening your hand to receive. Many people say "I would give if I were rich." This is false because if you cannot give a dime out of a dollar, then you surely would not give $100,000 out of a million.

Even if you do not have money, you can give in other ways. You could give your time by volunteering at a homeless shelter or cutting an elderly neighbor's grass without charge. You could also donate clothes and other goods you no longer need or use. If you are working, then you can give 10 percent of your income. Giving away $1 out of $10 would not be a harsh burden. Giving puts good karma in the air. It is best to give without the expectation of receiving something in return. Any type of giving is virtuous, but giving anonymously is most honorable. The satisfaction of knowing you made a difference in someone's life is priceless.

Donating and volunteering also relieves you of stress. What you do to others you actually do for yourself. What you give comes back to you like a boomerang.

When you are helping to fix the world's problems it makes your personal problems seem smaller and easier to conquer. You will gain a whole new perspective on life. Real problems consist of homelessness, hunger, lack of health care, lack of education, lack of clean water, natural disasters, etc. We are here on this earth to make a difference. Give generously like the wealthiest people in the world. Warren Buffet, Bill Gates, and Michael Bloomberg have all made pledges to give away the majority of their billions to charitable causes. Mark Zuckerberg pledged to give away 99 percent of his shares in Facebook stock.

CHAPTER 5

HOW TO ATTRACT MONEY

If you constantly focus on money, then money will come. Money loves attention. The masses usually don't think about money until they run out of it. Money will multiply if you treat it well. Don't worry about how you will arrive at your financial goal. The opportunities and information you need will line up for you at the right time. All you have to do is believe and take massive action.

The $10 Million Check

In 1990, world renown actor Jim Carrey was a struggling young comic trying to make a name for himself in Hollywood. One day while sitting on the top of a hill in his old car, he dreamed of a better future. He wrote himself a check for $10 million and wrote in the notation line "for acting services rendered." He dated it for Thanksgiving Day November 23, 1995. He kept that check in his wallet for years. In 1994, Jim Carrey's faith and hard work paid off. He was paid approximately $7 million to star in the movie *Dumb and Dumber*. He earned $20 million for *Liar Liar* in 1997 and $25 million for *Bruce Almighty* in 2003. Jim Carey is a perfect example of how the law of attraction works when you believe and stay the course.

Mind Your Money

Money making opportunities are always around you and they will become easily noticeable if you pay attention. You will attract money making opportunities when your mind is constantly focused on money. When I was in my early 20's, I decided I wanted to purchase a Corvette. I would fall asleep visualizing myself behind the wheel. I began to notice more Corvettes on the road than ever before. I was able to purchase a Corvette 2 years later. My Corvette purchase was not the most prudent financial decision at the time. However, it is just another example of what you continually think about will ultimately be reflected in your life. This also works for attracting money making opportunities.

In my early 30's I decided to focus on investing and financial freedom. Once my mind was tuned to money, I began to notice many different ways to invest and make my money grow. My money increased dramatically simply because I gave it more attention. Money is like a plant. If you ignore it, then it will die and wither away. If you give it plenty of water and cultivation, then it will grow and blossom. The law of attraction works the same for anything you want to flourish in your life. This power can be used for something meaningful or for something frivolous. Keep your mind tuned into meaningful objectives.

Work Smarter, Not Harder

Simply working hard will not make you rich. Janitors and waiters work very hard, but they ordinarily do not become wealthy. No matter how much overtime employees work, they will never make as much money as the owner of a company. A bartender will never make more than the owner of the restaurant. Business owners can play golf on weekdays while their employees drive in rush hour traffic stressed about being late for work. The majority of people who work on a job live paycheck to paycheck. They falsely believe that working overtime or getting a second job will improve their financial situation. Working hard at trading your time for a paycheck is not the best way to earn money.

Working hard is good, but you have to work hard in a certain way. Elite wealth builders work hard at discovering great investment opportunities and growing businesses. You should also work hard at developing your skills to become more valuable in the marketplace. The more skills you have; the more money you will attract.

Get in The Zone

When you are in the zone, money will start to flow from many different sources. Everything has a cause and effect. The financial seeds you planted will begin to grow. I have received checks in the mail and dividend payments from investments I completely forgot about. Be patient, because it usually takes 5 to 10 years of consistently sowing seeds of wealth before you become a money magnet.

Most people lose focus and patience and therefore will never attract significant money. Most people will quit if the money does not come instantaneously. People are addicted to immediate gratification. The best things in life always take time to develop. A gourmet holiday dinner takes hours to prepare. A stale frozen dinner only takes minutes to heat in the microwave oven.

Words Are Powerful

The masses often make statements that are based on a poverty consciousness. When they are running low on money they say things like "I'm broke" or "I can't afford it." People repel money and attract more inadequacy when such negative statements are made. Repeat affirmations such as "I am a millionaire" or "I am thankful for my great wealth that is increasing every day." You must say your affirmations with conviction and a smile on your face! Uttering affirmations will help persuade your subconscious mind that you are already rich. Say your words with passion!

The subconscious mind absorbs everything it hears and will magnetize what you program into it. Conduct an experiment by imagining yourself eating a lemon. Notice how your subconscious mind will make your mouth salivate from the memory of how lemons taste. The subconscious mind will believe whatever you tell it. Words precede any great achievement. Before a man walked on the moon, somebody said, "We can build a space shuttle that will fly among the stars." Never underestimate the power of your words.

Vocalize statements of gratitude every day when you wake up in the morning. Gratitude attracts more good things into your life. If you have a functional brain and an able body, then you are already rich.

Feel Comfortable with Money

Carry an appropriate amount of cash on hand. Having close access to cash will give you a feeling of abundance. Having physical cash on hand or in your home helps you develop a relationship with money. You need to feel comfortable with having large amounts of money readily available to you.

Wealth creation is an art and a science. Read as many books as possible about self-made millionaires and their personal routes to prosperity. Stay up to date with global financial news. Follow websites such as *www.wealthmotivation.com* for ideas and strategies to build wealth. Once you adopt a wealthy state of mind, you will start attracting and meeting wealthy people. Attend social events where prosperous people gather. Become accustomed to affluent environments and let it soak into your consciousness. When you are constantly around wealthy people, you will begin to think like they think and live like they live. Changing your circle of financial influence is critical.

Go to business conferences and seminars as much as possible. Attending a seminar is one of the easiest ways to surround yourself with like-minded ambitious people. I can guarantee there is a conference or seminar coming to a city near you. Conferences based on real estate, wealth management and technology are good places to meet and learn from other accomplished people. You can also find thousands of free webinars on the internet. You must feel as if you have already reached your financial goals. You have to feel and act as if you already have financial freedom. Walking, talking, and thinking like a wealthy person will draw money to you.

CHAPTER 6

BUILDING WEALTH IN THE STOCK MARKET

The financial markets have created more wealth than any other industry in the world. The majority of billionaires can attribute their source of wealth to the financial industry. Many hedge fund managers make more money in one year than your favorite athlete, actor, or musician will earn in his or her entire lifetime. In 2012, David Tepper, a hedge fund manager, personally made an estimated $2 billion. There is no limit to the money you can make in the financial markets. You don't need any social connections or formal education to open a brokerage account and participate in the financial markets.

No one can suppress your success based on your gender, race, age, or religion. You have full control of your destiny. Everybody has the opportunity to build wealth in the stock market. It's not enough to just save and leave your money in the bank. Inflation will eat away at your savings every year. You have to make your money grow and work for you. Today, it is easier than ever to invest in the stock market. You can set up a brokerage account online without having to meet with anyone.

The internet has given the individual investor more control and information than ever before. Investing can be a very emotional business. The more you control your emotions the more successful you will be. Common people only like investing when the economy is doing well, but the most money is made during recessions when stock prices are at their lowest. When you invest, do not invest with money that you need in the short-term. The stock market works best for people who have a long-term vision. Invest with an outlook of at least 10 years or longer. Give your investments time to grow. The stock market is not for a person with a get rich quick mentality.

Money that is correctly invested will work and grow while you are sleeping. Anytime you can increase your net worth without physically working is a good thing. Participating in the stock market allows you to buy assets that will increase in value over time instead of material items that will become worthless over time. Investing is a business. The basis of every successful business is diligent work, patience, research, forecasting, consistency and thinking outside the box.

Wealthy People Take Risks

To be successful at anything in life, you have to be a risk taker. There is never a great reward without risk. If you want to enjoy a vacation in Hawaii, you have to take the risk of flying in an airplane. As long as you are flying with a respectable and experienced airline, then you are taking an intelligent risk. However, you should always exercise caution. Investigate and do your research. Sometimes a risk can be too high and is not worth taking. You would be taking an irresponsible risk to fly with an unknown airline piloted by a Captain who is not licensed and properly trained. Everybody takes a certain level of risk just by walking outside of the house. If you never took any risk, you would have to huddle up in the corner of your bedroom and never leave; and there are people with agoraphobia who are actually afraid to go outside. You would be safe and secure, but you would not have a very productive or enjoyable life.

Just as you must take risks with your life, you must also take risks with your money. Your money will never grow if you just hide it underneath the mattress or keep it all in a traditional bank savings account. Money has to flow and circulate, in order to have value.

If your muscles remain inactive without exercise for a long period, you will lose your strength and good health. Everything in nature must continue to be in motion in order to thrive. If you don't use it, you will lose it. Never allow your money to remain stagnant for too long, because it will lose its value.

Circulating a portion of your money in the stock market is one of the best ways to allow your money to grow.

The Global Economy

The future is bright for the global economy. Nothing can stand in the way of human progress and innovation. American based corporations continue to attract the best and brightest talent from all over the world. The smartest students from around the globe travel to study at American Universities. Many of these high tier students work for American based companies after graduation. When you invest in American companies, you are essentially investing in the world. Most major corporations are global entities.

When it comes to business, America still has one of the most productive economies in the world. The internet is still young and American based corporations continue to be at the forefront of technological innovation. The future of the world is bright and you should profit from the progress. Investing in the stock market will allow you to capitalize on global economic prosperity. As the countries of the world continue to prosper, the stock market will ascend higher over the long-term.

Keep an investment eye on Africa. The continent of Africa currently has the most growth potential of any region in the world. American and

Chinese corporations are investing billions in Africa. Africa is the next frontier for explosive growth. Africa currently has the world's youngest and fastest growing population. The continent is home to more than 200 million people between the ages of 15 and 24, and its young population is increasingly well-educated.

Long Term Investing Will Make You Wealthy

The stock market has always gone up over the long-term. People accumulate wealth when they consistently invest and do not allow temporary market setbacks to discourage them. Over half of Americans do not invest in the stock market. One of the major reasons many people are left behind financially is because of their lack of participation in the stock market. Many people were frightened out of the stock market during the recession of 2008. Instead of panicking and selling at a loss, the recession of 2008 was the perfect time to put even more money in the stock market.

The Dow Jones Industrial Average more than doubled in value between the years of 2009 and 2014. In March 2009 the Dow Jones Industrial Average was around 7000 and by March 2014 it was over 17000. There has always been stock market bubbles and stock market crashes. The people who create wealth are people who invest on a consistent basis. It is wise to be an aggressive buyer of stocks during an economic downturn. When people are frightfully selling, you should be courageously buying. In 2000, there was a market crash caused by the internet stock bubble. In 2008, there was a market crash caused by the housing bubble. People who courageously invested during either of those market corrections made enormous profits.

You Can Become a Millionaire!

Throughout stock market history, the average yearly return for periods of 25 years or longer has been around 10 percent. The typical person in America currently spends around $500 a month on car payments. If someone invests $500 a month in a total stock market index fund that averages a 10 percent annual return, he or she would have about $1,031,400 in 30 years. Thirty years may sound like a long time, but it really isn't. Thirty years are going to pass by anyway, so you might as well become a millionaire in the meantime. You will become wealthy if you invest in appreciating assets, instead of depreciating liabilities such as expensive clothing and a new car every few years.

The majority of Americans who work forty years or more do not come anywhere close to reaching millionaire status. Most people will not have enough financial security to retire comfortably by age 65. You can choose to be different than the masses. If you have the opportunity to earn money in one of the wealthiest countries in the world, you should have financial security to show for your labor. The majority of American millionaires became rich through saving, investing, and living below their means. People who invest $500 a month in a total stock market index fund will have the pleasure of watching it steadily grow over the long-term. You can at least get the process started with $100 per month and you can invest more as your income increases. Something is better than nothing. The average person will waste over $100 a month on unnecessary shopping and fast food dining. Get started now and develop the habit of investing. Investing a little every month is a great wealth building strategy. This is called dollar cost averaging. It eliminates the stress of trying to time the market and picking the best point of entry. The longer your time horizon, the less risk you will have. The stock market has always gone higher over any twenty-year period.

Short-term volatility will make the value of your portfolio go up and down, but daily fluctuations is nothing but background noise. If you are a true long-term investor it does not matter what your portfolio does tomorrow, next week or next month. Give your assets time to grow. Daily fluctuations are not important.

A parking lot attendant in an eastern seaboard city makes $12 per hour and has accumulated more than $500,000 through saving and consistently investing in the stock market. They call him Mr. Earl. He also paid off his mortgage and sent his three children to private school. Mr. Earl never made more than $25,000 a year during his lifetime. He habitually invested in index funds and blue chip companies that paid dividends. Mr. Earl demonstrates that no matter how much money you make, you can still become financially secure by consistently saving and investing. If he can do it, then you can do it. Invest like Mr. Earl and allow your money to work for you.

Build Intergenerational Wealth

It is very simple to create a family legacy of wealth and freedom. If you have a long-term perspective beyond yourself, your grandchildren and great grandchildren will be swimming in excessive financial abundance. If you invested $10,000 in an index fund averaging a 10 percent annual return and let it grow for 100 years, it would be worth about $138,000,000. You would not have to invest another penny beyond the original $10,000. After 125 years, the portfolio would be worth over $1 billion. A $138 million portfolio would produce about $5.5 million per year with a 4 percent dividend yield. A $1 billion portfolio would produce about $40 million in annual dividends with a 4 percent yield. Your heirs could live off the dividends and never have to touch the principle. This is how the cycle of generational economic mediocrity can be changed. A billionaire family can be created from a mere $10,000. The power of interest compounded over the long-term is amazing. Think long-term and change the future of your family tree. Consult with a Lawyer about setting up a family trust.

Municipal Bonds

Municipal bonds can provide an excellent source of tax-free passive income every month. A Municipal bond is a debt security issued by a municipality, county or state to finance its capital expenditures. Municipal bonds are exempt from federal taxes and from most state and local taxes. State or local governments offer municipal bonds to pay for special projects such as roads, sewers, playgrounds, schools and bridges. Municipal bonds are usually safe investments. The default rate in most states and municipalities have been historically low. It is wise to make sure your municipal bond investments are diversified among states and communities with robust economies.

It is very easy to invest in municipal bonds through an exchanged traded fund. They can be easily traded like stocks with most brokerage firms. There are many different municipal bond funds that you may want to consider. Buying municipal bonds will not make you rich overnight, but consistently accumulating shares will provide you with dependable monthly income. The more shares you accumulate, the bigger your income will be. Every municipal bond fund has different attributes. It is important to do your own research to see which fund works best for you.

Exchange Traded Funds

I have made significant gains investing a portion of my money in exchange traded funds (ETFs). An ETF is a security that tracks an index, a sector, a commodity or a basket of assets; but it trades like a stock on an exchange. Some of the most popular ETFs are ones that mirror major stock market indices such as the S&P 500 and the Dow Jones Industrial Average. ETFs are great for beginning investors because they carry less risk than individual stocks. Individual stock ownership requires regular monitoring and analysis. The fundamentals within certain individual companies can change, which will require you to reassess your investment every quarter when they report earnings. You don't have to worry about quarterly earnings with exchange traded funds like you do with individual stocks.

Let's suppose you were interested in investing in technology stocks. You could purchase an ETF that contains a basket of several of the best technology companies. You would not have to rely on a single company to do well. Investing in an ETF is like buying the whole basket. There much research that goes into picking an individual company. If you are not hands on and do not have the passion to research individual companies, then it is best to invest in an ETF.

The Basics of Buying Individual Stocks

Let us assume you want to buy shares in ABC Corporation. If you purchased 100 shares of ABC Corporation at the assumed market price of $50 per share, it would cost $5,000. Multiplying the number of shares you want (100) by the market price of $50, is how you arrive at the cost to purchase the stock for $5,000. After you buy ABC Corporation and the price goes from $50 to $65, you will have made $1500 profit if you elected to sell. If the price goes down to $35 after your purchase, you will have a $1500 loss; but the loss will be realized only if you decide to sell. You never realize a profit or loss unless you sell. You can hold a stock as long as you want. If ABC stock pays a $2 annual dividend, then the company will pay you $200 per year for being a shareholder. $200 is derived from multiplying the number of shares you own (100) by the annual dividend of $2 which would be a 4 percent yield. The more shares you purchase over the long-term, the larger your dividend income will become. Many people lose money because they panic and sell as soon as they see a stock go down in value; which is why it is vital to do your research and only invest in a company that you believe has a good business model. When you are confident in your research, you will be more patient and let a stock rise in value. You won't panic and sell at a loss just because it loses value in the short-term.

Dividend Aristocrat Stocks

I prefer to invest in companies with a track record of increasing their dividend payments for 25 years or more. These types of stocks are called dividend aristocrats. Many of these dividend paying companies have been in business for nearly a 100 years or more. Many of them increase their dividend payments by 10 percent or more per year. Dividend aristocrats usually persevere during tough macro-economic conditions. I especially like consumer staples and utility companies. Consumer staples are essential products that people are unable or unwilling to cut from their budgets regardless of their financial situation. Items such as food, beverages, household and personal goods are always in demand no matter how the economy is performing. People will always need to buy soap, toothpaste, napkins, deodorant, laundry detergent, lotion, etc. Many utility companies such as electric and water firms pay reliable dividends. No matter how the economy is performing, there will be a steady demand for water and electricity. The majority of my capital is invested for dividend income and long-term capital gains. The majority of my holdings include ETFs, REITs and dividend aristocrat stocks.

Dividend aristocrat companies pay dividends on a quarterly basis to shareholders. Dividend payments reward shareholders with passive income as they wait for the stock to increase in value. I don't worry about short-term price movement in dividend aristocrat stocks. If the price temporarily goes down, then I can buy more shares at a discount and my dividend income will increase. When the stock price goes up, then the value of my portfolio increases. I win either way. Many people rely on dividend payments as an extra stream of income and hold particular stocks forever. Receiving a dividend payment is passive income at its finest. Building up a dividend portfolio over a long period of time has helped many people become wealthy. After many years of saving and investing, I know people who were able to quit their jobs and live primarily off their dividend income. It is better to be a long-term investor than a short-term trader. Don't be in a rush to become rich. Many people have become wealthy over the long-term by owning shares in solid dividend paying companies.

Invest in What You Understand

Some of the most successful investors attribute much of their success to investing in businesses that are easy for them to understand. If you have the desire to invest in individual companies, then I recommend conducting research on companies you are familiar with in your daily life. Stay away from companies if you do not clearly understand their business model. Don't invest in a glorified company just because they have a new technology that will allegedly change the world. You also do not want to invest in a company simply because an analyst on TV set a buy rating on the stock. If you don't completely understand the operation of a business and the revenue sources, then stay clear. In the late 1990s, many investors lost money from investing in unprofitable internet companies whose business model they did not understand. Only invest in what you know.

What products or services do you use regularly? Which company makes the detergent you use to wash clothes? What brand of toothpaste does your family use? Which waste company picks up the trash in your neighborhood every week? Which company produces your favorite bottled water or juice? Who is your electric and gas company? It is prudent to invest in familiar companies. Those are just a few examples of how you can incorporate investing into your everyday life. Everyone's life is different. There are many publicly traded companies that affect your life on a daily basis. Invest in simple businesses with high barriers to entry that provide products and services people always need. Investing in stocks doesn't have to be complicated. Keep it simple.

Using Technical Analysis

If you have determined that the fundamentals of a company are good, you should also look at the technical stock charts to examine which direction a stock is headed. Technical analysis is a methodology for forecasting the direction of a stock price through the study of past market data. There are many books and websites geared towards learning how to read technical indicators. I always examine the stock charts of individual corporations and ETFs when evaluating a potential investment. It can be very helpful to look at technical indicators before investing your money. There are many different technical indicators available. I use the MACD (moving average convergence divergence oscillator). It is a simple and effective momentum indicator.

Technical indicators can assist in helping someone pick a stock or an index fund at the best possible price point. It is ideal to buy an asset when it is consolidating sideways and getting ready to break out to the upside. Technical indicators can display when the asset's price is trending up, down or sideways. Technical indicators help mitigate risk.

Become Richer During a Recession

Recess means to take a break. An economic recession is when the economy is having a temporary period of economic decline. Just because the economy goes into a slump and lacks energy and ideas doesn't mean your personal finances have to decline. You don't have to slow down because others slow down. A recession is boom time for intelligent investors. You should be brave when everyone else is panicking. A recession is not real unless you believe it is. In the middle of the great recession of 2008-2009, there were still people creating products, seizing opportunities and becoming rich. Asset prices are the lowest during economic slowdowns. This is the best time to start increasing the value of your portfolio. Buy assets at low prices and sell them at higher prices when the economy recovers. Economic declines don't last forever.

Money is never lost; it is only transferred into other people's hands. All you have to do is think the opposite of the masses and put yourself on the correct side of the wealth transfer. Recessions come approximately every 7 to 10 years and are tough to endure. A recession will test even the strongest resolved investor. A recession comes fast and furious, but usually won't last much longer than 6 to 18 months. The 2000 and 2008 economic downturns were unforgettable. The financial news media made it seem like it was the end of the world.

Don't listen to the financial news for any serious advice or information. I can remember when so called experts on a financial news networks were advising people to buy a house at the top of the housing bubble in 2007. Financial news networks are for pure entertainment. During a recession, the majority of professionals on TV will advise you to sell at a loss and put your money underneath a mattress. The natural trajectory of the market has always been higher over the long term. Major stock market declines are buying opportunities.

Remember, it is wise to keep it simple and invest in a total stock market ETF and/or very high quality dividend aristocrat blue chip stocks. You will definitely know stock prices are the cheapest and the biggest profits will be made if you buy during an economic recession when the masses are terrified.

CHAPTER 7

GOOD HEALTH AND LONGEVITY

The greatest wealth is health. – Virgil

A person needs excellent health in order to live life to the fullest. You can successfully accomplish all of your goals and have a billion-dollar net worth, but your life cannot be fully enjoyed if you do not have excellent health. Good health is the foundation of life. Good health is also one of the most important keys to attracting abundance and living your life's purpose. You are a limitless soul that lives in a sacred body. You only receive one body to live in during your lifetime. You are obligated to take care of it and keep it pure. You can't trade your body in for a new one. Never take your health for granted. Having good health is mostly in your control. Maintaining a healthy diet and making good lifestyle choices will allow you to live a long life. It is never too late to begin eating healthier and improving your lifestyle.

It is possible to live for more than 100 years if you take care of yourself. Everyone is born in this world to complete a unique mission and to have a positive impact. You never know how long it will take you to fulfill your major purpose in life. Your major calling in life could take until you are 95 years old to complete. Even if you fulfill your calling at an early age, you will want longevity so you can enjoy the fruits of your labor. One of your major goals in life should be to live as long as possible.

Imagine the impact you can have on the world if you extend your life by an extra 50 years. We all have an impact to make on the world. The majority of deaths and illnesses are related to poor diet and lifestyle. In 2010, a study at the Center for Disease Control (CDC) showed that people are 10 times more likely to die from heart disease or cancer than from accidents or violence. The risk of heart disease and cancer can be lowered if you partake in nutritional eating habits and an active lifestyle. Most major ailments are preventable. Only around 30 percent of Americans eat the recommended daily intake of fruits and vegetables. Many people adopt sedentary lifestyles and poor dietary choices, which stimulate many diseases people are afflicted with today. If a person is raised in a household that encourages nutritious eating habits and exercise, then he or she will practice a healthier lifestyle into adulthood. Your quality of life is important. You need to be full of vigor, energy, and independence while you are alive. You do not have to be dependent on prescription medications and frequent doctor visits as you grow older.

Living a Healthy Lifestyle

Successful people understand the importance of healthy living. If you drive through most affluent neighborhoods, you will see people walking dogs, jogging, bike riding, playing tennis, practicing yoga, etc. You will also notice the abundance of healthy restaurants and organic grocery stores to choose from. Very rarely will you see unhealthy fast food dining options in affluent zip codes. This is not by accident; the market gives people what they want. High achievers are always looking for ways to preserve good health. Staying active and eating healthy has a big impact on their overall success in life. The great news is that every person can make the same healthy choices irrespective of his or her socioeconomic status. Anyone can decide to eat healthier and become physically active.

Nutritious Food Is the Key to Good Health

Let food be thy medicine and medicine be thy food.
-Hippocrates

Nature's medicine is derived from the food you eat.

Your body is naturally programmed to heal itself and fight off illness. The body needs the proper fuel from nutritious food to heal itself and function at an optimal level. Nutrient dense food, energizes you mentally and physically. Your brain is an organ and it also needs proper nourishment. If you want to reach your highest potential, then you have to be alert, focused, clear minded and energized. Your performance in life will skyrocket when you start fueling your mind and body with nutrient dense food. In spite of the typical unhealthy diet that most Americans consume, the average American usually lives to be about 75 years old. However, his or her quality of life may be poor and dependent on prescription drugs, which is not a good thing.

Just think how much longer Americans could live if they adopted healthier eating habits. The Japanese have the longest life span in the world. They are the most likely people in the world to live until 100 years old. Imagine how much more you can accomplish in your life by living 100 years or more! The Japanese diet is based on eating a lot of vegetables and minimal meat. When they do eat meat, they consume mostly fish. Vegetables are eaten with every meal in their diet. Japanese eat 5 times the amount of veggies than most Americans. The Japanese diet is not completely perfect. However, it would be wise to imitate how they make vegetables the foundation of their diet.

Fresh Produce

The healthiest food is located in the fresh produce department of your grocery store. Fresh fruits and vegetables should encompass the majority of your diet. Blending or juicing your fruits and vegetables is an efficient way of getting nutrients into your bloodstream rapidly. Try to consume most of your fruits and vegetables in raw form. The extreme heat from cooking depletes many of the nutrients and enzymes.

Stay away from processed foods. Anything that is processed and packaged is not natural for the human body. Common processed foods to avoid include refined sugar, artificial sweeteners, refined salt, breakfast cereals, potato chips, white bread, cheese, soft drinks, microwave popcorn, frozen dinners, etc. Fried foods should be avoided at all cost. Eating a lot of fried food increases the risk of stroke, diabetes, obesity, cancer and numerous other health problems.

Your consumption of meat products should be very minimal. The World Health Organization released a study declaring that processed meat such as bacon, sausage, hot dogs and other types of red meat significantly increase the risk of developing cancer. The human body does not require large amounts of animal protein. Many health experts believe there is more than enough protein in beans, nuts and green leafy vegetables to satisfy the body's requirements. Gorillas, Elephants, Horses, Giraffes and Bulls are some of the biggest and strongest animals on earth that only consume plants.

Consuming large quantities of animal products is not necessary for human strength and vitality. There are numerous examples of superior athletes who have performed at a high level without the consumption of animal products. Tennis superstars Venus and Serena Williams are Vegans. While eating a raw vegan diet, Serena Williams won the US Open in 2013. Olympic track runner, Carl Lewis adopted a Vegan diet to prepare for the world championship in 1991 when he ran the best meet of his life. Legendary NFL quarterback Joe Namath was a Vegetarian. Retired professional basketball player John Salley says he has never felt better since adopting a Vegan diet.

Lose Weight Now

Excess belly fat is hazardous to your health. The fat around your midsection creates toxins in your body. The vital organs in your midsection should not be surrounded by toxins. Large amounts of belly fat have been linked to many ailments such as diabetes, heart disease and certain forms of cancer. Having excess fat around the waistline should be taken seriously. Extra inches on your waistline signify potential health issues. A waistline of 35 inches or more for women is a cause for concern and a waistline of 40 inches or more for men could spell trouble.

Fortunately, you can lose extra pounds by adopting healthier lifestyle habits. Living healthy and controlling your weight is not a big mystery. The diet industry likes to make it seem complicated so they can sell you magic fat burning pills, protein shakes, and liposuction surgery. The best weight loss plan in the world is called WILL POWER. How strong is your will to stay healthy and live longer? Your body is your sanctuary. You are supposed to eat to live, not live to eat. Master your appetite, don't let it master you. The temporary pleasure from eating unhealthy toxic processed food is not worth the long term damaging effects. As time passes, healthy food will begin to taste good. Once your body is clean and detoxified, you will no longer desire harmful food. You will soon crave for a salad instead of a candy bar. You will prefer fresh strawberries instead of cookies.

Healthy food is processed naturally from the earth, such as fruits and vegetables. If it's from a fast food restaurant or processed in a factory, then it will usually be detrimental to your health. Maintain the discipline to eat what is good for you. Most people know that an apple is better than a donut, a salad is better than a hamburger, a banana is better than ice cream, and water is healthier than a soda.

Have patience and gradually transition to eating healthier. It will take time to wean yourself off junk food. Once you begin eating healthier, it will become easier to stay on the right path.

Six Super Foods

Coconut water

You can instantly feel the effects of how coconut water hydrates your body. It is healthier and more refreshing than any sports drink on the market. Coconut water has calcium, magnesium, phosphorus, potassium and sodium. It moisturizes your skin, lowers blood pressure and aids in weight loss. The meat inside a coconut is also delicious and healthy.

Cayenne Pepper

This is one of the best super foods on the planet. I endeavor to consume it every day in the powder form. You can instantly feel it boosting your metabolism and speeding up the digestion process. It is excellent for weight loss stimulation and the elimination of toxins.

Green Vegetables

Green leafy vegetables are great for aiding in digestion and elimination with its high fiber content.

It has increased levels of vitamin K which can help people suffering from Alzheimer's disease. It has antioxidants that help protect against various cancers. Kale can help lower cholesterol levels. Per calorie, kale has more calcium than milk, which aids in preventing bone loss, and preventing osteoporosis.

Watermelon

Watermelon is 92 percent water, but has many nutrients such as vitamin A, vitamin C, iron, and calcium. Watermelon contains antioxidants to help fight free radicals.

Berries

Berries pack an incredible amount of nutritional goodness into a small package. They're loaded with antioxidants, low in calories, high in water and fiber to help control blood sugar and keep you full longer. Blueberries are the best because they are among the best source of antioxidants and are widely available.

Lemons

Stay away from refined sugary beverages and drink water with a fresh squeezed lemon. Lemons boost your immune system, helps lose weight, clears the skin and provides energy. You can instantly feel lemons working to alkalinize your body.

Avoid Alcohol and Other Drugs

Drunkards and gluttons become poor, and drowsiness will clothe them in rags. - Proverbs 23:21

If you truly want optimal health and unlimited prosperity, then do not consume alcohol. Some people say that alcohol is okay to drink in moderation. It is actually best if you don't drink it at all. Alcohol has been proven to be a toxic substance. Therefore, it would not be wise to introduce your mind and body to any amount of toxicity. Alcohol is detrimental to vital organs such as the liver, kidney and brain. It is a perilous substance that could also lead to addiction. It is the most dangerous drug because it is legal and socially acceptable in most societies. It contains empty calories and sugar.

Alcoholic beverages will increase your appetite and make you more inclined to eat unhealthy processed food. It is difficult to maintain a healthy weight if you consume alcohol on a normal basis. Two bottles of beer have the same amount of calories as a sirloin steak. Two glasses of Gin have the same caloric intake as a Donut. One glass of wine is equal to eating four chocolate chip cookies.

This is why most habitual drinkers have bulging bellies.

Alcohol makes you lethargic and will diminish your mental sharpness. It is a low vibrational substance and attracts negativity into your life. It may give you a euphoric feeling in the beginning, but the long term effects are destructive to your personal relationships and professional productivity. Alcohol has destroyed many lives, families and careers. Alcohol and other drugs will mislead your decision making, deplete your energy and stifle your success. You need to have a clear and alert mind in order to reach your maximum potential.

Drink Water and Sleep Well

Drink plenty of water. Since the human body is comprised of approximately 70 percent water, proper hydration is paramount to good health. Health experts say you should drink half your body weight in ounces of water. If you weigh 150 pounds, then you should drink 75 ounces of water per day. Water is the ultimate body cleanser.

Also remember to get adequate sleep. Sleep is the period of time when your body repairs and rejuvenates itself. Adequate sleep keeps your immune system strong. Sleep deprivation will take a toll on your mind, body, and overall health. Make sure you get at least 7 hours of sleep at night.

Stay Active

Nutritious food is king and exercise is queen. If you combine the two of them together your body will be a kingdom. Staying active is just as important as eating healthy. At the minimum, you should walk 30 minutes every day. It is essential to keep your joints moving, blood flowing and muscles toned. Exercise also stimulates the brain and produces a euphoric feeling. Ask runners and weight lifters how good they feel after a workout. The easiest way to exercise is to find activities that you enjoy so it will not feel like a chore. There are many fun activities that can keep you active such as biking, skating, dancing, swimming, yoga, gardening, hiking, basketball, tennis, yoga etc.

Observe what happens to a car when it doesn't move and sits for an extended period of time. The battery will die, the brakes will corrode, and the tires will deflate. Nothing in nature is supposed to stand still. The earth rotates, trees keep growing and atoms are always moving. If you want to be in tune with nature, then you too must stay active. One of the reasons people become overweight, sickly and weak is because they have inactive lifestyles.

Good Thoughts = Good Health

A joyful heart is good medicine, but depression dries up the bones. - Proverbs 17:22

Out of a clean mind, comes a clean life and a clean body. – James Allen

Achieving optimum health is not only about exercise and nutrition. The thoughts you feed your mind are just as important as the food you feed your body. Optimal health is also related to preserving happy thoughts and low levels of stress. Your thoughts affect the cells in your body. Your body is a servant to your thoughts. It is important to maintain cheerful thoughts. Happy and pure thoughts will help you look younger and age gracefully. Never harbor evil or angry thoughts. There is always something in life to be thankful for.

Healthy and happy thoughts are like medicine. There is a strong connection between the body and mind. Fear and stress cause high blood pressure, headaches, stomach ulcers and premature aging. Maintain an optimistic mindset. Don't allow petty worries to stress you out. Most of the things people worry about will never happen anyway. Learn to smile more often. The more you smile, the happier you will feel. Make yourself smile and notice how your mood will automatically improve.

Hopefully, you have gleaned from this chapter the importance of good health so you can achieve your maximum potential in life. Continue to learn as much as you can about the subject of good health.

CHAPTER 8

GLOBAL TRAVEL

The world is a book and those who do not travel have only read one page. - Saint Augustine

The cave that you fear going into holds the treasure that you seek. - Joseph Campbell

Get out of your geographic comfort zone. In order to live a limitless life, you must travel and see different parts of the world. The world is your oyster. Countries and borders were created by man. Before there were countries, there was planet Earth. You are a citizen of Earth before you are a citizen of any particular country. You are not limited to one culture or one geographic region of the world. View life from a global perspective.

International travel will help you grow as a person. You will be able to understand the world from different viewpoints. If you are confined to one way of thinking, then you will not be a complete person. Your mental growth will languish. Living in one region of the world for too long only exposes you to one perspective. A lack of travel can lead to closed mindedness and complacency.

International travel will help you gain a lot of wisdom. Traveling within the confines of your own country is OK, but the character of your country is pretty much the same in each region with slight variations.

Only about 33 percent of Americans have passports. This is a mind boggling statistic. Everyone should have a passport. Owning a passport should be as common as having a driver's license. International travel allows you to take the best aspects of other cultures and blend it with your lifestyle.

The country of Japan has a technologically advanced economy. They think of success as more of a collective effort. If the team is successful, then everyone is happy. Individual achievement is not as important as their company, family and country. Honor and respect is everything. Japanese companies create products that are known for quality and dependability. Japanese automobiles are famous for being very reliable. Japanese culture exemplifies discipline and integrity.

The Latin American culture is very passionate, spiritual and friendly. Family is very important. They love culinary arts and dance. They are welcoming and sociable. They often acknowledge a stranger as a brother or a friend. It's important to learn from other cultures. Enhance yourself by incorporating the virtues of other societies into your life.

Profit From Traveling Abroad

The lessons I've learned from traveling to other countries have been priceless. In 2012, I visited several Latin American countries. At this time, a Canadian cellular phone company had lost popularity in the United States and its stock was crashing. Almost everyone in the USA was dumping this phone and switching to other brands. However, the Canadian company was still very popular in Latin America. The company still had some value left in its brand. This revelation compelled me to invest in their stock. I subsequently made a 100 percent return on my investment within two months. If I had never traveled abroad, I would not have obtained the wisdom I needed to make that profitable stock trade.

I know an American couple in the USA who envisioned retiring in a warm climate with beachfront property. They only had a nominal amount of retirement savings. Beachfront property in the USA was way out of their price range. Luckily, they had traveled a lot in the past and were open to living in another country. They realized they could live on the beach in places like Kenya, Philippines, Thailand or Costa Rica for a fraction of the cost in the United States. They probably would not have been open minded about cheaper international retirement properties if they had not been world travelers in the past.

Some people say they can't afford to travel. I say you can't afford not to travel. You will become a wiser person every time you explore a foreign land. Increasing your wisdom will increase your wealth. I know a guy from the USA who vacationed in a small Costa Rica beach town. He noticed the lack of fresh Mexican chipotle style restaurants in the area. He believed this would be a great business to start. He believed the popularity and success of fresh Mexican food in the USA could be duplicated in this small Costa Rica beach town. He eventually moved and opened up a restaurant. His restaurant was a grand success and provided jobs to many local residents. He is planning to open up more locations throughout the country. He would have not discovered this great business opportunity if he had not traveled internationally.

When you visit other countries, you should wander away from the hotels and tourist areas to spend time with the local people. You cannot learn anything new if you spend your whole trip confined in a resort. A five star resort in Brazil is going to feel the same as a five star resort in Orlando, FL. Venture into the local neighborhoods and learn about the culture. Most people who vacation at a resort in Cancun, Mexico do not learn anything about Mexican culture. They eat all day, go to the beach and party all night. Most tourists are afraid to go into the communities and intermingle with the local people.

Observing how people live in lesser developed countries can be very enlightening. Despite not having as many economic opportunities as industrialized nations, the majority of people in lesser developed countries are friendly, family orientated and enthusiastic about life.

I went to Southeast Asia on my first trip overseas. I met more new and interesting people during my two week stay in the Philippines than I had met in the last two years of living in the USA. The people were hospitable and easy going. The daily expenses in the Philippines were very low. I learned the value of enjoying life without the pressure of materialism. I was inspired to sell my new sports car and simplify my life when I returned to the USA. Material objects never provided me with the excitement I experienced on my trip in the Philippines. Experiences are more valuable than material objects. Material things come and go, but experiences last forever. Each of my international trips has had a tremendous impact on my life.

Learn a New Language

Everyone should learn more than one language. Studies show that there are many cognitive benefits gained from being multilingual. There are also many social benefits. People in other countries will respect and embrace you even more if you speak their native tongue. Your ability to make friends and network will be enhanced. A multilingual person will also have a competitive edge with business opportunities.

Staying Safe While Abroad

The majority of the people around the world are law abiding citizens. You have to be cautious and aware no matter where you are in the world. If you are respectful and use common sense, then you will be safe while abroad. The vast majority of people on earth will not bother you if you do not bother them. Use the same logic when it comes to safety as you would in your home country. Shy away from displaying jewelry, cash, and expensive electronic devices in public. There are some war-torn regions of the world that are not worth visiting. Beware of countries that have unstable governments and frequent terrorist attacks. Always check the Department of State website for alerts at your destination of choice.

Never Hesitate to Travel Alone

Many people agonize at the thought of traveling abroad alone. It is nice to have a travel partner to explore unknown territories of the world, but unfortunately it's not going to be feasible most of the time. Most of your friends will not have the money or time to travel with you. The majority of your trips abroad will have to be alone. You will find it very enjoyable wandering about alone. You will have more freedom to do what you want. While traveling, you will eventually link up with new people who have similar interests as you. Traveling is the best way to meet others who also like to travel. Global travel will connect you with some of the most interesting and successful people in the world.

CHAPTER 9

THE POWER OF BELIEVING

Life's battles don't always go to the stronger or faster man, but sooner or later the man who wins is the man WHO THINKS HE CAN! - Walter D. Wintle

When a politician is campaigning to become the president, he or she already has a presidential feeling inside. Before someone purchases a Ferrari, he or she has already imagined the feeling of driving behind the wheel of a super car. Before a person becomes a Millionaire, he or she already has the composure of a Millionaire.

Unshakable Confidence

Everyone has tremendous talent and potential. The one thing that holds most people back is self-doubt. It is not the lack of knowledge or ability that holds a person back, but the lack of self-confidence. When you go to sleep at night you do not doubt the Sun will rise in the morning. This is the same unwavering confidence you must have to accomplish your goals. What goal would you aim for if you were guaranteed success? Your   dreams are assured to happen if you truly believe. The only way you will be persistent is if you have unwavering faith. Expect to win in life. Expecting to win is what will wake you up early in the morning to continue working hard to accomplish your objective. Society will always try to set boundaries and limits for you. It is up to you to decide if those limits are real or not.

Faith will keep you focused on your goals and moving towards the prize. When you are intensely focused on your goal, adversity will go unnoticed. An Olympic hurdler never slows down when approaching an obstacle in a race. He or she simply jumps over the hurdles as if they were not there. Obstacles become practically invisible when you are vehemently focused on a goal.

When you believe you have already achieved your objective, it is then only a matter of time before it becomes a reality. What do you want? You are the creator of your own circumstances. Your current life is a reflection of your past desires that you believed were possible.

What you want in life, also wants you. Having unwavering belief is more important than knowing the specific mechanics of how you will achieve your objective. The universe will guide you on the right path towards completing your mission.

The biggest problem most people have is a lack

of faith and patience. Instant results are not realistic. A seed planted will not instantly bear fruit the next day. Respect the process of nature. Nature always takes its time. Do not terminate your progress if you don't see quick results. If your faith is resolute, your goals will become reality and there will be no limit to what you can accomplish.

Abundance is Yours

There is a magnificent power that dwells inside of you. Successful people believe in their innermost power to become prosperous. This belief gives them the confidence to make big plans and take massive action towards achieving their goals.

Never put limits on what you want out of life. The ocean does not care if you come with a spoon or a giant bucket. When you observe nature you will never see a shortage. There is an abundance of oxygen, water, trees, flowers, etc. Infinity is the essence of our Universe. Once you accept and truly believe this, you will be on the path to prosperity. You will separate yourself from the masses who believe in limitations. Everyone has a choice. Choose to embrace your power and enjoy a life of prosperity.

If you have good health and a sound mind, then you have no excuse for not achieving your goals. The masses refuse to cultivate their talent. If you waste your talent, you will always miss the mark.

Your talent is what will produce prosperity in your life. If you want a better life, work on yourself to become a better person. Never let your gifts and abilities lay dormant. You should continually grow and cultivate your skills. Repetition is key. The more you practice, the faster you will become great. It is your duty to make the most out of life and be all that you are meant to be. All things are possible when you believe in yourself and take consistent action. If you have unflinching faith, there is nothing you cannot achieve. The only person that can prevent you from accomplishing your goals is you.

Marc Hill

REFERENCES

Kirk Spitzer, aarp.org (May 2014) "Secrets From the longest-living Place on Earth". aarp.org. www.aarp.org/health/healthy-living/info-2014/longevity-secrets-from-japan.html

Heather Long, cnn.com (April 10, 2015) "Over Half of Americans Have $0 in Stocks" money.cnn.com/2015/04/10/investing/investing-52-percent-americans-have-no-money-in-stocks/index.html

Neilson.com, (May 20, 2009) "Americans Watching More TV Than Ever: Web and Mobile Video Up Too" www.nielsen.com/us/en/insights/news/2009/americans-watching-more-tv-than-ever.html

Dave Ramsey, daveramsey.com(August 24, 2016) "The Truth About Car Payments" www.daveramsey.com/blog/the-truth-about-car-payments

Drake Baer, businessinsider.com (October 22, 2014) "Most of The World's Billionaires Made Their Money In These 5 Industries" www.businessinsider.com/how-billionaires-made-their-money-2014-10

Editorial board, nytimes.com (October,28, 2015) "Meat as a Cause of Cancer" www.nytimes.com/2015/10/28/opinion/meat-as-a-cause-of-cancer.html

Ben Reynolds, gurufocus.com (June, 6, 2016) "How To Create Intergenerational Wealth" finance.yahoo.com/news/create-intergenerational-wealth-221631838.html

Joshua Becker, Author (May 3, 2016), "The More of Less: Finding the Life You Want Under Everything You Own"

Arnold Schwarzenegger, Author (November 5, 2013) "Total Recall: My Unbelievable True Life Story"

Matt McFarland, washingtonpost.com (March 24, 2015), "When Elon Musk Lived on $1 a Day"
www.washingtonpost.com/news/innovations/wp/2015/03/24/when-elon-musk-lived-on-1-a-day/

Oprah Winfrey Network (October 13, 2011), "What Oprah Learned from Jim Carrey | Oprah's Life class | Oprah Winfrey Network"
https://www.youtube.com/watch?v=nPU5bjzLZX0

Kelli B. Grant, usatoday.com (June 30, 2013) "Americans hate their jobs, even with perks"
http://www.usatoday.com/story/money/business/2013/06/30/americans-hate-jobs-office-perks/2457089/

Natalie Avon, cnn.com (February 4, 2011) "Why More Americans Don't Travel Abroad"
www.cnn.com/2011/TRAVEL/02/04/americans.travel.domestically/index.html

THE SECRET TO PROSPERITY